Images of Western Railroading

Steve Schmollinger

MBI

First published in 2003 by MBI Publishing Company, Galtier Plaza, Suite 200, 380 Jackson Street, St. Paul, MN 55101-3885 USA

© Steve Schmollinger, 2003

All rights reserved. With the exception of quoting brief passages for the purposes of review, no part of this publication may be reproduced without prior written permission from the Publisher.

The information in this book is true and complete to the best of our knowledge. All recommendations are made without any guarantee on the part of the author or Publisher, who also disclaim any liability incurred in connection with the use of this data or specific details.

We recognize that some words, model names and designations, for example, mentioned herein are the property of the trademark holder. We use them for identification purposes only. This is not an official publication.

MBI titles are also available at discounts in bulk quantity for industrial or sales-promotional use. For details write to Special Sales Manager at Motorbooks International Wholesalers & Distributors, Galtier Plaza, Suite 200, 380 Jackson Street, St. Paul, MN 55101-3885 USA

Library of Congress Cataloging-in-Publication Data Available

ISBN 0-7603-1574-4

On the front cover: Top: Milwaukee Road brakemen at Avery, Idaho, with two Little Joes and a GP9 in the background, July 31, 1973. *Bottom:* Santa Fe train symbol 991 in California's San Joaquin Delta, June 22, 1991.

On the frontis: In October 1995 on California's Donner Pass, a Southern Pacific unit grain train originating on the Union Pacific and operating with UP run-through power catches the last rays of the setting sun between Yuba and Emigrant Gaps.

On the title page: Leaving the flatlands and waterways of the San Joaquin Delta behind, Santa Fe's 199 train, the hottest symbol on the railroad, begins its climb over California's Coast Range at Martinez, California, in September 1985. In the distance stand the smokestacks of the Tosco Oil Refinery and Monsanto Chemical Plant, which the train passed 10 minutes ago.

Above: In August 1973, a set of Southern Pacific light helpers led by a General Electric U30C drifts downgrade on the approach to the Tehachapi Loop among lice oaks and dry grass. In the background stands Black Mountain, which has kept watch over the loop since it was built in 1876.

On the back cover: A Chicago-bound Santa Fe intermodal approaches Stockton Tower, February 1991.

Edited by Dennis Pernu
Cover designed by Tom Heffron
Interior designed by Mandy Iverson

Printed in Hong Kong

Contents

Acknowledgments		6
Chapter One	**Spanning the Great Divides**	8
Chapter Two	**Profiles from the West**	28
Chapter Three	**Railroaders at Work**	58
Chapter Four	**The Railroad Never Sleeps**	88
Chapter Five	**The Evolution of a Machine**	110
Chapter Six:	**Memories from the Mountains**	138
Index		168

Acknowledgments

Although virtually all of the photographs in this volume were taken by me, there are many people who had a hand in making this collection of images and text possible.

First of all, I would like to thank my wife, Lynn, for her unwavering support for my photographic endeavors. I would also like to thank my five children, Alex, Burke, Carlyle, Wyatte, and Mia, for their interest and participation in the quest to obtain ever-fresh images from along the rails.

Second, I would like to thank my parents, and especially my mother, for encouraging me to continue my photographic efforts. We tend to be our own worst critics, and my mother was able to see beyond my over-critical view, insisting that there was a spark of talent behind my work.

My sincere appreciation goes to Lynn Powell and Dave Stanley, two of my old-time sidekicks from the 1970s. Lynn and I made numerous trips to Donner Pass, the Feather River Canyon, Tehachapi, and Cajon, and in August 1972 traveled to British Columbia and Alberta. Dave and I spent time shooting Tehachapi and Cajon in 1973 as a warm-up for a trip to the Pacific Northwest and to see the Milwaukee Road's electrification in the Rocky Mountains. Several of the images from that trip to Idaho and Montana appear in this work. Thanks also go to Tom Barashas, who accompanied me on a trip to Empalme, Sonora, and Guadalajara, Jalisco, in May 1984.

For some of the technical information regarding motive power, thanks go to Max Ephraim, Jack Wheelihan, and Danny Johnson. Max was a chief design engineer for EMD in La Grange, Illinois, during its heyday, and his insights and experiences are priceless.

Jack was a senior district leader for EMD's Service Department for many years, and he brings a fresh—and boldly accurate—perspective regarding the reasons EMD did certain things, why certain locomotives were successes and others were failures, and so forth. Danny is a good friend, whose knowledge of prime movers comes as a customer of the builders, and thus he brings yet another perspective to the table.

Many thanks are also due the numerous railroad employees who were kind enough to share some of their experiences with me. Kenny Ball, Darrel Dewald, Wayne Ferrier, William Franckey, Doug Harrop, Jake Jacobson, Al Krug, Gene Lawson, Bill Plattenberger, and Dave Stanley all made significant contributions to the text of this volume. Also, I would like to express appreciation to Milwaukee Road historian Noel Holley for the knowledge and insights he contributed.

John Bromley, Union Pacific's manager of public relations, helped me gain access to the ex–Southern Pacific Roseville Shops and the ex–Denver & Rio Grande Western Burnham Shops in Denver, as well as to the ex-SP "Cape Canaveral" fueling facility in Roseville, and the ex-WP facility in Stockton, California.

Cesar Romero, chief engineer for the Ferrocarril del Pacifico, helped me obtain permission to take photographs at the railroad's shops in Empalme, Sonora, and Guadalajara, and also arranged a cab ride on the northbound *El Costeño* between Guadalajara and Tepic, Nayarit.

Mike Martin, who has since left the railroad industry, helped me get a cab ride on Santa Fe's 891 train between Barstow and Needles, California, with three brand-new red-and-silver EMD GP60Ms on the

Against the backdrop of a threatening afternoon sky in February 2003, a westbound Burlington Northern Santa Fe "Z" train loaded with time-sensitive truck trailers holds the mainline near Wagon Mound, New Mexico, as Amtrak train No. 4, the *Southwest Chief*, slides eastward through a siding. The semaphore signals in the foreground, long a fixture on western railroads, will soon be replaced by high-tech appliances.

point. Mike also provided me a letter of authorization to take pictures along the right-of-way in northern Arizona at a time when the railroad was conducting a dragnet in that area to catch a gang of sophisticated thieves from Mexico who had stolen numerous items from piggyback trailers.

I would also like to express appreciation to Ted Benson, whose reviews of my first and third books, *Tehachapi: Railroading on a Desert Mountain* and *Desert Railroading*, were quite complimentary. Such praise from one of this era's most noteworthy and respected rail photojournalists is extremely gratifying.

Sincere thanks also go to Kevin Keefe and Mark Hemphill of *TRAINS* magazine, Jim Boyd and Steve Barry of *Railfan & Railroad*, and Dale Sanders and Brian Rutherford of *CTC Board Railroads Illustrated* for their willingness to use my photos and stories in their periodicals, and thus spur me on to improve and expand my photographic and journalistic abilities.

Finally, I would be remiss if I didn't thank my Heavenly Father for His protection and prospering hand that has been operative throughout my life. I thank Him for my family, as well as any talents I might possess.

Chapter One

SPANNING *the* GREAT DIVIDES

I've barely had my Toyota RAV4 for a month, and here I am changing a flat tire. Must have picked up a nail or something along the right-of-way between Vail and Rita Road, where I now find myself with tire iron in one hand and flashlight in the other. But the flat tire isn't my biggest worry. Just east of my location is a giant "monsoon" storm cell, generating 40-mile-per-hour westerly winds and shooting lightning bolts earthward that I can sense are getting closer by the minute. While I'm changing the tire, my tripod and camera are staring the storm right in the face with the shutter locked open. An eastbound manifest passed about a half-hour ago, and the headlight of an eastbound "Z" train is just now becoming prominent down the long tangent toward Tucson. As it passes, even though it's only 20 yards away and fighting a significant grade, the roar of the Z's lead SD70M is largely muffled. The mayhem of the storm—thunder and blasts of wind mixed with ultraviolet light, dust, sand, and a few rain drops—make me glad when I finally plop into the driver's seat, start the engine, and roll safely out of harm's way toward home. For the residents of Vail, however, this is just another stormy August night.

Such is the nature of capturing images of railroading in the western portion of North America. It has its rigors, what with the rugged terrain, dynamic and sometimes fierce weather, and the long distances between traffic centers and concomitant infrequency of train movements. But it also has its rewards. To name a few, they take the form of diesel locomotives silhouetted against dramatic sunsets, passenger trains climbing through countless square miles of unspoiled timber; shiny steel rails that reach toward an open, jagged horizon to reveal the intensity of a headlight at dusk; and the sound of prime movers bouncing off steep canyon walls covered in a powdering of fresh snow.

There is more substance to western railroading, though, than mere aesthetics. Railroads helped build the West. In fact, without railroads, the development of the West would have been severely stunted, and even at this late date the region would suffer economically in their absence. The vast wild and largely unsettled regions of the three current partners of the North American Free Trade Agreement were populated in large part through the transportation on railroads of hopeful families and individuals into these areas in the nineteenth and twentieth centuries. California, the U.S. Southwest and Pacific Northwest, the Canadian provinces of British Columbia and Alberta, and the Mexican states of Sonora, Sinaloa, Nayarit, and Jalisco owe a substantial portion of their current economic vitality to the railroads.

Donner Pass and the Great Basin Desert

The first of the western railroads to span a major geographic divide was the Central Pacific. The foothills of the Sierra Nevada Mountains are not often identified with the Civil War era, but that's when the Central Pacific was battling it out with the lower reaches of Donner Pass. Having broken ground January 8, 1863, in Sacramento, the fledgling railroad constructed only 18 miles and made it to Junction (present-day Roseville) by the spring of 1864. Company officials had wanted to put on a grand display at the groundbreaking, but Collis Huntington rained on their parade by expressing his honest feelings: "Now, if you want to jubilate, go ahead and do it. I don't. Those mountains over there look too ugly, and I see too much work ahead of us. We may fail, and if we do, I want to have as few people know it as we can. And if we get up a jubilation, everybody will remember it. Anybody can drive the first spike, but there are many months of labor and unrest between the first and last spike."

Huntington's advice proved prophetic. The battle against the Sierra Nevada was monumental, but in the end, the Big Four—Huntington, Charly Crocker, Mark Hopkins, and Leland Stanford—and the men under their command rose to the challenge and completed a railroad through Donner Pass and across the Great Basin Desert.

Once the Big Four had built the Central Pacific, they took every precaution possible to protect and foster its interests. The vehicle they used to block the entry of competing railroads into California was the Southern Pacific Railroad. Eventually, the SP stretched from Portland, Oregon, to New Orleans via Los Angeles. The SP was also one of the first railroads to use the printed word to lure people to the territories it served as a way to build a traffic base. As Tomas Jaehn, curator for American and British history, Stanford University Libraries, describes, SP published a magazine that touted the wonders and potential of the West:

> To secure the continuation of revenues and profits after completion, Southern Pacific owners and their supporters turned into enthusiastic boosters and land developers. While some profits were sought in ferry and passenger train services, the Southern Pacific's larger objective was to develop suburban areas and, to a lesser extent, urban and rural regions throughout the West.
>
> Advertising was one way to increase visibility. Up to the 1890s, railroads typically limited advertising to running timetables in local newspapers. Railroads not only began to advertise heavily in magazines and other high-toned media, [but] the Southern Pacific decided to publish its own magazine. In May 1898, the Passenger Department created *Sunset* magazine, essentially as publicity for railroad lands and tourism. No outside advertising was accepted in the first few issues, as the Southern Pacific expected to underwrite the entire expense as part of its advertising program. In its

PREVIOUS PAGES: September 1974 on the double track at Cable in California's Tehachapi Pass. A Southern Pacific merchandise train carrying, among other things, lumber to help support the housing boom in the Los Angeles Basin, passes a short Santa Fe freight carrying truck trailers on 89-foot flatcars, otherwise known as "piggyback" trailers. SP EMD SD40T-2 8356 is barely two months old, and carries state-of-the-art radio gear in its "snoot," or short hood. The radio gear is used to control a "slave" SD40T-2, part of a swing helper, which is cut into the train about two-thirds of the way back.

first issue, at 5 cents a copy, editors promised their readers conveniently "information concerning the [Western states and territories]—a rich and inexhaustible field over which the dawn of future commercial and industrial importance is just breaking." *Sunset* directed its information primarily toward tourists, who were in the late nineteenth century, above all else, potential investors and migrants, and secondly to Westerners seeking economic improvement or recreational diversion. The magazine sold the West's best commodity, its environmental attractions and economic potentials, to thousands of men, women, and children.

For example, the February 1899 issue of *Sunset* described the route's premier passenger train, the *Sunset Limited*, in the following complementary terms: "The most perfect example of the luxury of modern railway travel. Equipment consists of Composite Buffet Library Car, Ladies' Compartment and Parlor Car, elegant Double Drawing-room Sleeping Cars and Dining Car."

Others who were familiar with the bounties of the region also published works extolling its virtues. For example, in an essay written for the U.S. Railroad Administration, the well-known author Zane Grey penned the following accurate description: "The secret of the fascination of the Southwest is exceedingly hard to define in words. But the secret of the health and renewed life to be found there seems to be a matter of the senses. That is to say, you must see, smell, feel, hear, and taste this wonderful country, and once having done so, you will never be the same again. It must be done to be believed. Never a one of the many people I have bidden ride over this region has failed to bless me for the suggestion."

Indeed, the blessings and bounties of the region had a great attraction, something well understood by William Simpson, who became general advertising agent for the Santa Fe Railway in 1900. Simpson offered trips to the Southwest to artists residing in the eastern United States in exchange for their renderings of the region's native peoples and landscapes. In time, the Santa Fe had hundreds of superb paintings from which to draw for its advertisements, calendars, and the covers of menus that graced its dining cars.

Marias, Stevens, and Rogers Passes

One of the great railroad men of the nineteenth century was John F. Stevens. After working as a civil engineer for railroads in Minnesota, Texas New Mexico, and Iowa, he joined the Canadian Pacific and worked his way up to division engineer, working the mountain passes of British Columbia. A few years later, he joined the organization of James Jerome Hill, known as the "Empire Builder," who was endeavoring to construct an unsubsidized railroad from the Great Lakes to Puget Sound. Stevens was appointed locating engineer for the railroad west of Havre, Montana, and in bitter cold weather on December 11, 1889, discovered the famous Marias Pass that allowed Hill's Great Northern Railway to cross the Continental Divide. He then explored the Cascade Mountains and the Columbia River to continue the railroad's progress toward the Pacific and located what is now Stevens Pass in Washington. To show its gratitude for Stevens' efforts in finding Marias Pass, the Great Northern erected a bronze statue of the engineer at the summit of the pass in 1925.

To the north lay the mighty Selkirk Mountains, with Calgary and the Canadian prairies to the east and Vancouver, British Columbia, to the west. The Canadian Pacific reached Calgary in 1883, but there it stopped for lack of a definite way through the mountains. In 1865, Walter Moberly and Albert Ferry pushed westward up the course of the Illecillewaet River, thinking it would lead to a pass through the Selkirks. The next year, Ferry, traveling without Moberly, turned back before he could confirm the existence of a pass. Perhaps an account of the privations that explorers in the Selkirks had to endure, written by Sir Sanford Fleming 20 years later, gives us an inkling of why Ferry turned around:

> The walking is dreadful, we climb over and creep under fallen trees of great size and the men soon show that they feel the weight of their burdens. Their halts for rest are frequent. It is hot work for us all. The dripping rain from the bush and branches saturates us from above. Tall ferns sometimes reaching to the shoulder and Devil's Clubs

through which we had to crush our way make us feel as if dragged through a horsepond and our perspiration is that of a Turkish bath. We meet with obstacles of every description. The Devil's Clubs may be numbered by millions and they are perpetually wounding us with their spikes against which we strike. We halt frequently for rest. Our advance is varied by ascending rocky slopes and slippery masses, and again descending to a lower level. We wade through Alder swamps and tread down Skunk Cabbage and Prickly Aralias, and so we continue until half-past four, when the tired-out men are able to go no further...."

Onto the stage of history came Major Albert B. Rogers, who was determined to find a pass through the daunting Selkirks for the Canadian Pacific. On May 29, 1881, 15 years after Ferry had retreated, Rogers, who was completely out of food, glimpsed the pass that would take the railroad over the mountains and on to Vancouver. In 1885 the Canadian Pacific was completed through Rogers Pass.

Ruta de la Costa Occidental

To the south, the Sud-Pacifico de Mexico (Southern Pacific of Mexico) did not begin building the *Ruta de la Costa Occidental* (West Coast Route) until 1905. Acting under the direction of E.H. Harriman, J.A. Naugle signed a concession with the Mexican federal government. The agreement granted the SP authority to construct a line from Alamos, Sonora, south through the cities of Culiacan, Mazatlan, Santiago, and Tepic, and into the Sierra Madre Occidental to a point "most convenient" on the Mexican Central Railroad, which would later become part of Nacionales de Mexico.

This "most convenient" point proved to be Guadalajara, but to reach it the railroad had to overcome some of the most formidable construction obstacles on the North American continent. On February 5, 1912, work was halted by the Mexican Revolution, but in 1923 the company reached an accord with President Alvaro Obregon. The railroad was partially compensated for damage done by revolutionary and federalist forces in exchange for a commitment to eliminate the 164-kilometer (102-mile) gap between Tepic and La Quemada within four years. This stretch included the area known as *Las Barrancas*, or "the canyons"—26 kilometers (16 miles) that would ultimately require 26 tunnels, 11 steel viaducts, and the lives of 16 men to complete. But with the muscle of thousands of Mexican *campesinos*, who worked with pick and shovel, wheelbarrow and basket to move untold tons of earth and rock, the SPdeM made good on its promise. Early on Friday afternoon, April 15, 1927, the entire line from Nogales to Guadalajara was completed with the driving of the final spike at the giant Salsipuedes ("Get out if you can") trestle, 860 feet above the floor of Las Barrancas.

Thus were the first transcontinental railroads established in Mexico, Canada, and the United States. They were the forerunners of other enterprises—Ferrocarril del Pacifico (which took over SPdeM's properties on December 21, 1951); Canadian National; Atchison, Topeka & Santa Fe; Union Pacific; Chicago, Milwaukee, St. Paul & Pacific; and Western Pacific, as well as "granger" roads and regionals such as the Chicago, Rock Island & Pacific and the Denver & Rio Grande Western. Of all these major names, only CN and UP survive today, but the last 30 years of western North American railroading have brought more than nominal changes to its milieu. The pages of this volume capture some of those many changes, as well as the flavor that is unique to railroading in the West.

LEFT: Testing to make sure its prime mover is operating properly, Western Pacific mechanical forces at Oroville, California, notch out the throttle of BN Alco C636 4365 on a clear day in December 1972. In a few hours, the big Alco will be headed up the WP's Feather River Canyon on a merchandise train headed for the Pacific Northwest.

Filling the air with typical Alco exhaust, three ex–Northern Pacific RS11s help an EMD GP38-2 speed through the eastern portion of the beautiful Columbia River Gorge at Towal, Washington, in August 1973. The track was part of the Spokane, Portland & Seattle Railway, which along with the Chicago, Burlington & Quincy, Great Northern, and Northern Pacific, was merged into the Burlington Northern Railroad in 1970. The ex-SP&S mainline runs on the north bank of the river, while that of the Union Pacific runs on the south bank.

RIGHT: BN train 137 arrives at WP's Stockton Yard on a beautiful afternoon in May 1973 as WP power is serviced at the diesel facility. A good portion of the inbound train's consist will soon be hauled to the WP–Santa Fe interchange tracks, where it will be switched into a Santa Fe train headed for the Los Angeles Basin. The BN-WP-ATSF relay from the Pacific Northwest to Los Angeles and vice versa was designed to compete with SP's one-carrier service between Portland, Oregon, and California's Southland.

Spanning the Great Divides 13

A General Electric Dash 8-32BHW leads a westbound Amtrak *San Joaquin* passenger train past a Santa Fe work extra led by a B23-7 at Oakley, California, in March 1997. The passenger diesel is decked out in the special California Department of Transportation's (Caltrans) dark blue, silver, and gold paint scheme, since Caltrans foots most of the bill to fund the San Jose–Bakersfield *San Joaquins*.

Trailing a plume of black diesel smoke as it helps lift a piggyback train toward Southern California's Cajon Summit, Santa Fe GE U36C 8706 fills the air with a loud, staccato exhaust. The hot westbound "pig," which momentarily will pass through the small town of Hesperia, will terminate at the railroad's Hobart Yard in Los Angeles.

LEFT: A few minutes after the sun has lifted above the northeastern horizon, Santa Fe train symbol 991 tiptoes over the wooden trestle between the drawbridge at Orwood and the span at Middle River. In the distance, fog from the coast skirts the base of Mount Diablo on the crisp summer morning of June 22, 1991. Within a year, most of the timbers of this mile-long structure in the middle of California's San Joaquin Delta will have been replaced with pre-stressed concrete.

Thundering up Tacoma Hill, a Milwaukee Road southbound freight behind three GE "U-boats" begins the journey to Portland, Oregon. Cut into the train two-thirds of the way back is an EMD F7 A-B-B-A helper. The big manifest will use home rails for part of the trip, and then switch to BN's mainline for the rest of the journey via trackage rights obtained when BN was formed.

Milwaukee Road's premiere westbound transcontinental freight train, the *XL Special*, glides downhill along the bank of the St. Joe River on a crystal clear day in August 1973. In a few miles, the train will arrive at Avery, Idaho, for a crew change. Avery, a quaint little railroad village nestled in the Bitterroot Mountains, was located at the western end of the railroad's electrification that stretched across Montana and Idaho.

A pair of the biggest diesel locomotives in railroad history, along with an EMD GP9B, roars up the eastern slope of Cajon Pass in April 1974. The Union Pacific's DDA40X sported two prime movers rated at 3,300 horsepower each and many innovations, such as modular electrical components that were tested and later featured as standard equipment in EMD's Dash 2 series of locomotives.

Thick, dark clouds form a menacing backdrop as one of UP's 1,100-odd EMD SD70Ms and a pair of GE Dash 9s depart Tucson, Arizona, on a "monsoon" afternoon in July 2002. The sunshine will disappear in only a moment, replaced by a downpour and lightning as the storm looses its full fury over the Sonoran Desert.

18   Chapter 1

On June 14, 1989, Denver & Rio Grande Western's train 144 rounds the horseshoe curve above Gilluly, Utah, on its way to Denver, Colorado, and points east. In its assault of Soldier Summit, the train has already wended its way through Gilluly's first two horseshoe curves. With a ruling mainline grade of 2.4 percent, the climb to Soldier Summit is one of the steepest in the United States.

A combination of D&RGW EMD SD40T-2s and SD50s pull 10,000 tons of Utah coal up the eastern slope of Soldier Summit at dusk in June 1989. Although the relatively small D&RGW had recently merged with the far-flung Southern Pacific, D&RGW power was still the rule here on the regional's home rails.

Having just departed Nacionales de Mexico's patios (yard) on the south side of Guadalajara, an EMD hood unit hauls empty mill gondolas toward Mexico City. The rail the train is plying is welded, and the ties it sits on are concrete—features which even some U.S. mainlines could not boast of in May 1978.

It's 1 P.M. in May 1978, and Ferrocarril del Pacifico's train No. 1, *El Costeño*, departs Guadalajara Union Station bound for Nogales, Sonora, just south of the Arizona-Mexico border. The train is more commonly known as *La Bala* (*The Bullet*), and thanks to Montreal Locomotive Works and Alco, it has plenty of power on the head end for the 1,200-mile journey that lies ahead through some of Mexico's most rugged terrain.

In an unseasonable July storm in the Sierra Nevada Mountains, Amtrak's train No. 5, the *San Francisco Zephyr*, rolls downhill through Dutch Flat, California, in 1974. The two EMD SDP40Fs, purchased new by Amtrak in 1973 and 1974, form a sharp contrast to the hand-me-down passenger equipment they have in tow.

22   *Chapter 1*

With ex-SP EMD FP7 6451 on the point as helper for the trip over the Sierra Nevada, Amtrak's eastbound *San Francisco Zephyr* grinds uphill through Yuba Gap in January 1973. As a cost-cutting measure, SP removed one of the two main tracks here in the summer of 1994. However, doing so greatly reduced dispatchers' operating flexibility on Donner Pass.

With the beautiful mountains of British Columbia for a backdrop, a Canadian Pacific manifest makes its way west toward Vancouver in August 1972. Power on the train is a Montreal Locomotive Works M630, followed by two GMD SD40-2s. MLW is Alco's Canadian affiliate, while GMD is EMD's.

24   Chapter 1

Two Fairbanks-Morse H-16-44s bring a Canadian Pacific freight across the Columbia River near Trail, British Columbia, in August 1972. The railroad's F-M "C-liner" cab units, which for some time held many an assignment on this secondary mainline, have recently been silenced for good.

Canadian Pacific's crack transcontinental passenger train, *The Canadian*, is about to duck into a tunnel near Lake Louise in August 1972. The sheer beauty of the Selkirk Mountains and the wonders of Banff National Park are surely enough to keep most of the passengers' peering through the streamliner's windows on this dynamic afternoon in the Canadian Rockies.

Spanning the Great Divides 25

In October 1973, an eastbound WP freight sporting a block of Western Fruit Growers Express reefers approaches the Santa Fe diamond at Stockton Tower in central California. No. 3068 East is headed for the Inside Gateway to the Pacific Northwest via the WP's High Line, which begins at the left leg of the Keddie Wye, deep in the Feather River Canyon.

SP 9803 West departs Roseville Yard at Antelope in September 1994 with the sun lying on the horizon. The manifest's conductor is still busy looking over his paperwork, having boarded the train only a few minutes ago on the bypass track that runs around the western edge of the yard. More power will be added to the train at Bakersfield to increase its horsepower-per-ton ratio for the run over Tehachapi and Cajon.

Chapter Two

PROFILES
from the
WEST

There are many facets to railroading in the West. Laden with history and legend, the region is boundless in its variety of tales and landscapes. Here and in the rest of this chapter, vignettes from the West set railroading in various contexts.

At the beginning of the twentieth century, a crude pathway from the Midwest to Los Angeles began to form along the Santa Fe Railway and other railroads. In the next 20 years, automobile booster clubs pieced together stretches of passable roadway along the path and called it the Old Trails National Highway. Cyrus Avery of Tulsa, Oklahoma, and John Woodruff of Springfield, Missouri, promoted the idea of a paved road linking Chicago and Los Angeles, and their efforts ultimately bore fruit in the form of one of the most famous of all highways in the world. Officially designated Route 66 in the summer of 1926, only 800 miles of the new roadway were paved at that time. Beginning in the Depression year of 1933, thousands of unemployed young men from all over the United States labored in gangs to blacktop the final stretches of the highway. Thanks to their efforts, the road was completely paved from Chicago to L.A. by 1938.

From the beginning, public planners wanted Route 66 to link the main streets of communities, including those in the Southwest, so those towns could be part of a major thoroughfare. The highway became one of the country's main east–west arteries, and its climate, which was temperate compared to more northern highways, made it especially popular with truckers. Besides the "Mother Road," the famous thoroughfare also became known as the "Will Rogers Highway" and "The Main Street of America." It tied the Southwest together in a way that only the railroads had done up to that time.

The major metropolitan area at the western end of Route 66 was Los Angeles. After the Atchison, Topeka & Santa Fe arrived in L.A. in 1887, the city's population boomed. From 11,000 in 1880, it jumped to 102,000 in 1900, 577,000 in 1920, and 1.3 million by 1930. Through its expanding workforce, attracted in part by Southern California's beautiful climate and an excellent harbor, the city's industrial production exploded in the 1920s.

During the Dust Bowl years of the 1930s and 1940s, hundreds of thousands of people traveled west on Route 66 in search of a better life, accelerating the population growth in the Los Angeles Basin, as well as in the southern San Joaquin Valley in and around Bakersfield. During World War II, the government invested billions of dollars in capital projects in the Los Angeles area, creating thousands of jobs, many of which were filled by people who arrived via the Mother Road. The highway allowed truckers to compete with the rails, but it also helped expand the markets the AT&SF served on its "Coast Lines." As time passed, hundreds of gas stations, restaurants, "motor courts," and motels sprang up along the highway, many of which are still in business today.

Over the years, as air travel took hold in North America, the famous streamliners that once graced the rails faded into ragged forms compared to their once-sleek images. Finally, in May 1971, virtually all long-distance passenger train service in the United States was transferred from the Class I railroads to the National Railroad Passenger Corporation, or Amtrak. In its early days, Amtrak ran some noteworthy "rainbow" consists comprising equipment from several different carriers. A good example was the fledgling agency's transcontinental streamliner running between Chicago and Denver on the Burlington Northern as the *Denver Zephyr*, then to Ogden, Utah, via Cheyenne, Wyoming, on the Union Pacific, and from there on to Oakland, California, via the Southern Pacific. Amtrak's timetable of November 14, 1971, assigned its Denver–Oakland train Nos. 5 and 6 and gave it the name *City of San Francisco*. On June 11, 1972, Amtrak renamed its train running the entire Chicago–Oakland route the *San Francisco Zephyr*. On April 25, 1983, shortly before the train began using the Denver & Rio Grande Western between Denver and Salt Lake City, it became the *California Zephyr*.

In June 1973, Amtrak assigned several ex–Union Pacific E-units, still in their original paint, to the pool from which the *San Francisco Zephyr* drew its power. The Es joined 14 ex-SP FP7As and five F7Bs already in the pool and still wearing scarlet and gray, and were joined shortly thereafter by new EMD SDP40Fs. In time, many of the Es and Fs received Amtrak paint and were transferred to other routes. Nos. 5 and 6 often added a helper at Reno and Roseville, usually a single SP SD40 or SD45 on the point.

At the time Amtrak came into being, the Southern Pacific was on the threshold of a buying spree in which it would purchase hundreds of new EMD SD45T-2s and, later, SD40T-2 Tunnel Motors. SP had already bought hoards of conventional SD45s and, to a lesser degree, SD40s to handle tonnage over its many mountain districts, including Donner Pass between Roseville, California, and Reno, Nevada. Donner's numerous tunnels and snowsheds, coupled with its stiff grades, had helped spawn the unique Tunnel Motor design. SD45s and SD40s sported air intakes that did not have sufficient capacity to cool the prime mover once the locomotive was out of the bore or enclosure; passing through a close succession of tunnels and sheds caused their engines to overheat. The Tunnel Motor design featured substantially larger air intakes situated lower on the locomotive, helping to solve the overheating problem.

PREVIOUS PAGES: The sun is setting over the Sonoran Desert as an eastbound Union Pacific intermodal train approaches the west switch at Wymola, Arizona, in April 1999. Much of the western United States is dominated by sparsely populated arid lands. However, in recent decades, even these wastelands have given rise to giant traffic centers, such as Las Vegas, Phoenix, Tucson, and Salt Lake City.

About the same time SP was buying 20-cylinder diesels in the late 1960s and early 1970s, the Milwaukee Road was still using electrics a half-century old to cross the Cascades and Rocky Mountains. Gene Lawson, retired engineer from "America's Resourceful Railroad," recalls an exceptional experience he had running the old motors:

> The most memorable experience I ever had while running the electrics was on a trip somewhere around 1970. I was called for locomotive E-25 in Othello with a tonnage train to go to Beverly, and double the train to Kittitas. When I arrived at Beverly, I saw three or four men with cameras and sound equipment while I was setting out the first half of our train on the passing track. We then went to the mainline and coupled to our train. I was pumping up the air on the first cut of cars when a gentleman named Don L. Hunter, a professor at the University of Oregon Audiovideo Media Center, came up and asked if he and his crew could ride with us. I said "yes," as it was Sunday and no one was around. I told them to ride in the cab on the rear end of the locomotive, but don't go back into the unit, and they said they would not. It really turned out to be an historical trip. They took many pictures and recorded all the sounds. Those sounds are now copyrighted material and are used in the WB Video Productions *The Milwaukee's Mighty Electrics* videotape. When we left our first cut at Kittitas, I didn't change ends to go back to Beverly with the light engine, so they had a bird's-eye view from the east end of the locomotive on the return trip.
>
> Other than an occasional problem with a bearing, the electrics never ran hot. In starting a train, before notching out to full series, it was in "resistance," and when you pulled the throttle to cross over to "parallel," it would be back in resistance until you got all notched out to full parallel. You had to notch out fairly fast so you wouldn't overheat the resistor grids. At the point of crossing over from series to parallel, the locomotive would kind of jerk a bit, but not enough to do any damage to the train. It would command your full attention. To start regeneration after just tipping over the top of a mountain grade, I would leave the throttle in full parallel. Then I would reach just above the throttle to the regenerative braking control and bring it out one notch to the equalizing notch, and wait until enough of the train began pushing us and the pulling of the amps dropped to zero. Then I would notch out and watch the amps go over to braking. I would then listen to the gears humming, which was like music to my ears. Too bad we don't have the electrics today—no pollution at all! The regenerative power went back into the Northwest Power Pool.

Wayne Ferrier, another Milwaukee man who worked the Coast Division, remembers, "The old adage was that the power fed into the trolley going down the grade was enough to power a train going up the hill on the opposite side. This was not true."

Railroading in the West has been built on the character of men and women like Lawson and Ferrier, a tradition that holds true today. Lowell S. "Jake" Jacobson, a man who appreciates the value of positive PR as much as the bottom line—and understands the connection between the two—may be the best-known railroader in the country, even though he operates an obscure little shortline in southeastern Arizona. From well-known industry journalists to humble seekers of a few trackside photos, Jacobson shows uncommon warmth toward anyone with a genuine interest in the operation he and his people run virtually 24 hours a day, every day of the year. The Copper Basin Railway runs 60-car trains of copper sulfide ore between ASARCO's Ray Mine complex and its Hayden smelter; a "unit" train of sulfuric acid and cone settler overflow, a.k.a. "mining liquor," to the pit for leaching copper from oxide ore; and a Florence local that interchanges copper anodes and other loads with Union Pacific at Magma Junction.

As with many shortlines, the Copper Basin has limited resources, but Jake and his compadres squeeze all they can out of them and then some. An example of CBRY's homespun frugality is its rail-replacement program. Jake inherited a property that consisted of nothing but jointed rail, mainly 113-pound with scant few 136-pound, between Ray Mine and the Hayden smelter. Some of the rail was even as light as 75-pound between Ray Junction (where the line to Florence diverges from that to the mine) and Magma Junction through the scenic Gila River Canyon. In 1995, Jacobson poured $3.7 million into rail upgrades, which included replacing the archaic iron in the Ray–Magma segment with used 136-pound steel from the Santa Fe. On average, the railroad replaces 3 miles of track annually at a cost of about $1.5 million. All track between Ray Junction and the smelter is now 136-pound, continuous welded rail.

To get every ounce of worth from its rail, the CBRY will take a section of track that's been used up on one side and move it to the opposite side of the track to take advantage of the life left in it. Once it wears down on that side, the only other place to get more use from it is in a tangent, where it can be worn top-down. But because the CBRY doesn't have many tangents, a good number of these "sticks" end up on the scrap heap. Fellow railroaders know better than to buy used equipment from Jacobson, since the CBRY sucks every ounce of productivity out of its equipment and rail before giving it up.

Such are just a few of the many portraits of the railroads and railroaders of the American West.

In April 1974, a trio of Phase I SDP40Fs drop off the western slope of Cajon Pass west of Devore, California, with the *Southwest Chief*.

In 1973 and 1974, newly formed Amtrak took delivery of its first brand-new locomotive, the EMD SDP40F. For reliability and fuel economy, Amtrak chose EMD's 16-cylinder prime mover rather than the 20-cylinder version, which had received a black eye due to weak A-frame welds. The cowled locomotive also had the same modular components as those used in the SD40-2. The locomotives performed almost flawlessly until 1976, when they were involved in major derailments on the Louisville & Nashville and the Burlington Northern. The source of the problem was thought to be their hollow-bolster, high-traction (HTC) trucks, but this was never proven conclusively. However, by 1982 Amtrak had traded in most of its SDP40Fs for new four-axle F40s, making it one of the shortest-lived locomotive batches of all time. In July 1974, two SDP40Fs on Amtrak train No. 6, the *San Francisco Zephyr*, have just met a pair on their opposite number at Rocklin, California, during an odd, midsummer storm.

Owing in part to the fact that three major Class I railroads crossed in its shadow, and in part because Winterail is held in Stockton, California, Stockton Tower was a favorite spot for rail enthusiasts until it was demolished on May 27, 1999. The tower operator controlled movements on the Santa Fe (now BNSF), Southern Pacific (now UP), and Western Pacific (now removed) mainlines, and could be heard on radio scanners for miles around. By night and by day, the tower stood as a landmark of western railroading activity. As part of its press for greater efficiency, BNSF closed the tower on January 12, 1999, and turned traffic control through the plant over to its dispatcher in Fort Worth, Texas. A further diminution of the crossing's importance came when UP tore out its ex-WP mainline through Stockton in 1999. Now it's only a piece of ground with hardly a trace of the tower left behind. In March 1990, the "gumball machine" on the roof of an SP Tunnel Motor leading a westbound leaves a trail behind at the tower, shortly after a vigorous storm left puddles throughout the area.

With hot cargo bound for Los Angeles, SSW 9628 West crosses the Santa Fe under the watchful care of the tower operator in September 1996.

In Guadalajara, Jalisco, in April 1978, a Ferrocarril del Pacifico switch crew using an RS3 brings a string of second-class passenger cars down to Union Station.

LEFT: Almost every railroad in western North America purchased products of the American Locomotive Company, or Alco, during its early days of diesel building. Its locomotives were based around a 244 prime mover, a reliable four-stroke machine that endured thousands of hours of intense use. Hundreds of S-class switchers and RS-class road switchers worked yards, transfer runs, and road freights, with their distinctive gurgling sound echoing off the tops of the rails. They all had a rounded cab with several large windows on their sides, front and back, giving operators a clear view of brakemen, railcars, and wayside signals. A switch crew huddles on the front of an ex–Spokane, Portland & Seattle RS3 in July 1973 at Willbridge, Oregon. BN 4070 still had a few good years left in her.

Three Santa Fe S2 switchers idle between assignments in February 1973 at the railroad's San Bernardino Yard in Southern California.

Profiles from the West 35

An excellent railroad on which to observe four-cycle railroading in the 1970s was the Ferrocarril del Pacifico. Stretching from Nogales, Sonora, at the border with Arizona, to Guadalajara in the heartland of Mexico, the former Southern Pacific of Mexico threaded its way through some of the most challenging mountains in the Western Hemisphere, skirted the Pacific coastline, and crossed the hottest desert on the continent. Riding the railroad's premiere passenger train, *El Costeño,* was an adventure never to be forgotten. Pullman sleepers from the New York Central and other U.S. roads made up the consist that often burgeoned to 22 cars or more. Power was a combination of big Alcos, Montreal Locomotive Works, GEs, and even some smaller units when the need arose. Despite being absorbed into the Ferrocarriles Nacionales Mexicanos, the FCP has left an indelible, progressive mark on western Mexico. In June 1978 at Guadalajara Union Station, a trio of NdeM GP38s cuts off of *El Tapatio* as an MLW M636 and Alco RSD12 prepare to head north with FCP's *El Costeño.*

36   Chapter 2

An unconventional passenger consist by U.S. standards, two MLW M420TRs and a U30B back down onto the point of *El Costeño* early in the morning in June 1978.

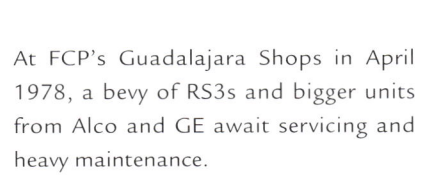

At FCP's Guadalajara Shops in April 1978, a bevy of RS3s and bigger units from Alco and GE await servicing and heavy maintenance.

GP38 9237 leads NdeM's passenger train to Manzanillo on the Pacific coast out of Guadalajara in June 1978. Next to the baggage cars is a home-built coach.

LEFT: Although Nacionales de Mexico was somewhat of a staunch customer of EMD, it also had some very interesting operations in Guadalajara. The nationalized carrier used a combination of mostly EMDs and a handful of Alcos and GEs to move trains in and out of Mexico's second largest city. Although not run as efficiently as FCP, NdeM had at its disposal resources that Pacifico couldn't match. NdeM was thus able, for example, to install continuous welded rail on its double-track mainline, as well as some concrete ties, two attributes that were still somewhat novel in North America in the 1970s. On a relatively clear morning in May 1978, despite heavy particulates cast into the air from *la zona industrial* in the southern part of the city, *El Tapatio* enters a big rock cut a few miles south of Union Station. It's behind a pair of high-hood GP38s sporting a consist that looks like a page from U.S. passenger railroading in the 1950s.

An EMD SDP40 pushes hard behind the caboose to assist an NdeM southbound freight up the hill just south of the carrier's Guadalajara *patios*, or yard.

Profiles from the West 39

RIGHT: Resting on the turntable tracks in Stockton on an overcast afternoon in January 1974, two of WP's final four F7As wait for their next assignment west over Altamont Pass in the Coast Range.

Almost as interesting as any railroad south of the border, Western Pacific had an operating philosophy that was distinct from the lines that surrounded it. The railroad purchased only four-axle power, although it ran pooled six-axle units from BN and UP. WP maintained its locomotives in almost flawless condition, and subsequently had very high unit availability. The railroad advertised its services—both for freight and passenger—in such periodicals as *Time*, *Newsweek*, and *National Geographic*. Early on, the entire railroad from Salt Lake City to Oakland was placed under the control of dispatcher-operated Traffic Control System machines, or TCS. Its somewhat flamboyant orange-and-silver paint scheme, inspired by hues found in the Feather River Canyon, was a breath of fresh air when compared to the drab garb employed by neighboring railroads. In a sentence, the WP was a classy operation. At sunset in May 1973, a freight from the east has just pulled to a stop at the west end of Stockton Yard. At right, a Baldwin VO-1000 makes up a train headed for Salt Lake City.

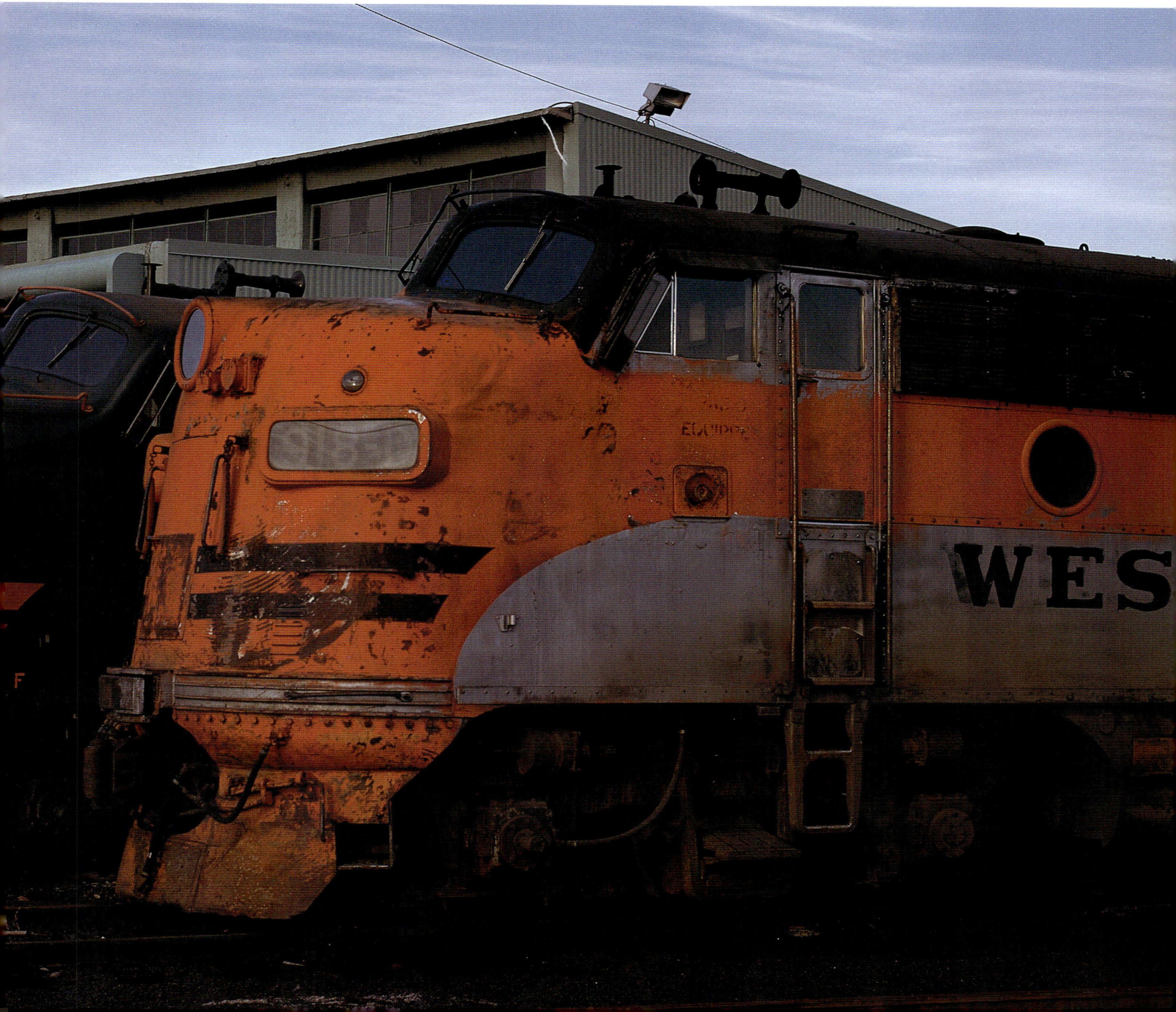
WES

RIGHT: SP's San Francisco Peninsula commuter trains were for a time graced with Fairbanks-Morse Trainmasters, big 2,400-horsepower diesels that had an elegance all their own. SP purchased F-M Trainmaster demonstrators Nos. TM-3 and TM-4 in 1953, and took delivery of 14 more Trainmasters the following year. They were first assigned to the Sunset Route out of El Paso, Texas, but were reassigned to commute service in mid-1956. Their opposed-piston prime mover yielded tremendous acceleration, making them perfect for getting out of a station quickly, getting up to speed, and then slowing for the next station. Their out-of-the-station exhaust was a telltale white instead of the usual black, and their superstructure was simple and sleek, with huge six-axle trucks that had a 13-foot wheelbase, a single-equalized design, and roller bearings. They were equipped with Nathan M5 horns and a large Pyle oscillating light to get motorists' and commuters' attention. With their powerful prime mover, which was ahead of its time, they could pull long trains, like train No. 126 headed for San Jose behind Trainmaster No. 3029 at South San Francisco in March 1974.

The nose of SP Trainmaster No. 3031 at San Jose, California, in July 1972, shows its Nathan M5 horn, large oscillating light, and smaller fixed headlight.

42   *Chapter 2*

BELOW: At SP's Bayshore engine facility in April 1974, a mechanic has the top off of 3025's engine compartment to gain access to the prime mover. Meanwhile, EMD SDP45 3200 is being returned to service after receiving some vital repairs.

43

Tehachapi Pass in California is probably best known for the loop laid out by Southern Pacific's chief engineer, William Hood, in 1876. A lesser-known fact about the pass is its beauty in springtime. When winter rains reach their normal amount, the months of February, March, and April are spectacular in the Tehachapi Mountains. As winter gives way to spring, green grass appears on all of the mountains and hills, covering them in an emerald green. Then come wildflowers, adding splashes of red, orange, yellow, and purple to the verdant scenery. On the western slope, tender green leaves appear on the oak trees that dot the hillsides, and later deep red blooms appear on the prickly pear cactus. Sunshine makes the days warm, but nights are still chill. Early in the morning on April 26, 1985, Santa Fe 5050 East, a 971 train, roars through the giant horseshoe at Allard, surrounded by the greenery of the Tejon Ranch.

In April 1992, with purple wildflowers covering the slopes of the hills at the east end of Cliff siding, two EMD GP60s scream as they help lift an 11,000-ton eastbound coal train headed for the ovens of North American Chemical Corporation in Searles, California.

44   *Chapter 2*

In April 1974, two of the biggest diesels ever to grace the rails bring a UP merchandise train into one of the last curves before reaching the summit of Cajon Pass. The five-year-old Centennials were the brainchild of the railroad's chief mechanical officer, Dave Neuhart. At a time when reports from the field indicated that customers wanted higher reliability rather than more horsepower, Neuhart was somewhat of a rogue. But UP's formula for staying competitive was long runs at high speed with gobs of tonnage. Locomotives with thousands of horsepower, like the Big Boys and the Challengers that preceded them, were one good way to do it. Max Ephraim, an engineer who joined EMD in 1939, recounts that the locomotive builder was usually pretty good at anticipating customers' needs. "However," he adds, "with the recent 'H' engine, UP actually came to EMD and told them 4,000 horsepower was not enough." Nobody's perfect.

Leading a train north out of Stockton on ex-WP trackage in June 1997, 80-foot EMD SD9043MAC 8047 is one of 369 such units in UP's fleet. To date, it is the largest single-engine diesel-electric ever constructed.

Profiles from the West   45

In 1969, the year that Alco ceased building locomotives in the United States, Canadian Pacific was in the midst of taking delivery of 59 M630s from Montreal Locomotive Works, the Canadian firm to whom Alco had sold its locomotive designs. The M630s were big, brawny four-cycle machines noted for their pitch-black exhaust when revving up. Their turbochargers were exhaust-actuated, which meant that the prime mover's drive shaft had to reach a certain rpm before the black smoke abated. An example of this is shown in a view of an eastbound CP manifest in British Columbia in August 1972. By the time the smoking MLW reaches us, its exhaust will have begun to dissipate. The M630 sported a 251—a 16-cylinder, "V" prime mover with an air starter. They were initially assigned to the mountainous western subdivisions, working between Calgary, Alberta, and Vancouver, British Columbia, but were later assigned to the eastern portion of the system. While in the West, they made for an impressive sight while pulling coal trains—such as 4570 and 4559 (right) rolling a drag westbound at Spuzzum, British Columbia—or while just sitting—like 4507 (far right) at Coquitlam, British Columbia, in August 1972, resplendent in the railroad's maroon, gray, and yellow paint scheme.

46   Chapter 2

Profiles from the West 47

In 1983, after coming to the conclusion that they could not survive against the fierce competition of the UP—which had gained direct access into Northern California via its purchase of the WP—SP and Santa Fe decided to merge. On December 23, 1983, they combined their holding companies and placed the SP in a voting trust pending Interstate Commerce Commission approval of the marriage, which the companies were sure would come. Santa Fe was so confident that the merger would go through that its chairman authorized the repainting of hundreds of locomotives in the new SPSF image scheme, which comprised elements and colors of the two companies' liveries. Santa Fe GE C30-7 8090 (above) models the SPSF paint scheme at Muir, California, in Franklin Canyon. The merger unit has a 943 train bound for Chicago in its wake on April 22, 1989. The ICC rejected the merger in 1987 due to its "anti-competitive" attributes. A decade later, Santa Fe and Burlington Northern, which actually had much less overlap than Santa Fe and SP, successfully merged and developed a paint scheme that combined "heritage" colors and facets of the Great Northern, a BN predecessor, and the Santa Fe. In September 2002, BNSF freights pass west of Darling, Arizona, with a pair of GE Heritage II Dash 9s leading the eastbound (right).

48   Chapter 2

Profiles from the West 49

Running down a city street in Renton, Washington, in August 1972, a Milwaukee Road freight from the Midwest heads for Tacoma behind an EMD GP40, FP45, and SD40-2.

Even after the Milwaukee Road discontinued its electric operations on the Coast Division in 1970, it was still worthy of observation in Washington and Oregon. With the fateful BN merger that same year, it had gained access to Portland, something it had been seeking for decades. "America's Resourceful Railroad" wasted little time exploiting its new traffic center, and established close ties with the SP to gain access to the Oregon and California markets. The Milwaukee captured upward of 80 percent of the total traffic out of the Port of Seattle, and almost 50 percent of total traffic out of the Pacific Northwest. Milwaukee also gained a large portion of the automobile traffic via a new 133-acre loading facility opened in 1969. In summary, traffic on the Pacific Extension was burgeoning even as it fell off on the Milwaukee's "granger" lines in the Midwest—the Milwaukee Road was kicking BN in the pants in terms of long-haul traffic. To power its trains between the West Coast and St. Paul and Chicago, the railroad used a variety of four- and six-axle power, including EMD GP40s, SD40-2s, SD45s, and FP45s, and from GE, everything from U25Bs to U36Cs. An example of such a consist is seen entering Tacoma Yard from the east in August 1972, with a GP40 leading an FP45 and three SD45s. Although the revenues from the Pacific Extension were soaring, the railroad's management didn't plow a good portion of the profits back into the property to revitalize ballast, track, and other critical facilities, or to buy new freight cars to handle expanding traffic. Little by little, the track structure literally eroded away from under the trains that passed over it, the carrier turned away business for lack of cars to ship it in, and the Extension became untenable. It was one of the greatest travesties to occur in North American railroading.

Late in the evening in July 1973, a local behind GP40 2058 rolls through Maple Valley, Washington, with several loads of woodchips for one of the paper mills the Milwaukee Road serves.

Like the Milwaukee Road, the Denver & Rio Grande Western had to compete head-on with titans to survive. As a result of the 1982 merger of the UP, Missouri Pacific, and Western Pacific, the D&RGW gained trackage rights into Kansas City, Kansas, via the ex-MoPac east out of Pueblo, Colorado, but little else. By using its access to the Kansas City gateway and forming an alliance with SP, the Grande attempted to build long-haul traffic. On February 2, 1986, the carrier initiated its *Railblazer* service between Denver and Salt Lake City, with only a single crew change at Grand Junction, Colorado. But the coup de grace occurred on August 9, 1988, when the ICC approved the purchase of the far-flung SP by the relatively small D&RGW. It was like the mouse eating the lion. The combined railroad, known as Southern Pacific Lines, then purchased the St. Louis–Chicago portion of the Chicago, Missouri & Western, which the ICC also approved, giving the railroad a system that reached from the nation's hub at Chicago all the way to the West Coast. But it was all for naught. Southern Pacific Lines could not compete with the UP or even with the Santa Fe, which had the shortest and fastest route to Chicago from California. Thus, corporate machinations and necessities obliterated the distinctive Rio Grande, like so many railroads before it. On June 30, 1997, the proud D&RGW was formally merged into the giant UP system. On June 12, 1989, a Rio Grande Tunnel Motor (above left) leads three SP units along the Colorado River at DeBeque, Colorado. Later that afternoon, another D&RGW Tunnel Motor (left) charges west with a manifest as the shadows at DeBeque lengthen.

In 1986, EMD released three four-axle demonstrator locomotives to the Santa Fe for testing. They were dressed in a blue-and-white scheme with silver trucks, and had an SP-type lighting package complete with a red "cherry" in the nose. Developing 3,850 horsepower, they were the B-B incarnation of the builder's SD60, which it had released two years earlier. Subsequent sales were somewhat less than impressive, with only four railroads purchasing them. What EMD had failed to realize was that, first, its competitor, GE, was quickly gaining market share with its Dash 8 line, and more importantly, that orders for new four-axle power were on the way out in North America. UP had set the trend by purchasing nothing but C-Cs since 1989 and ordering a boat-load of SD60s, SD60Ms, and Dash 8-40Cs. Six-axle power, UP claimed, was easier on its track, and the four extra traction motors gave the C-Cs the edge in flexibility; they could be used in heavy-haul service as well as on high-speed intermodal trains. Far and away the biggest buyer of GP60s was SP/St. Louis Southwestern (Cotton Belt), taking delivery of 191 of them over a number of years. Sales of the SD60/SD60M were substantially greater, with UP alone taking 366. So, despite how good EMD GP60 demonstrators 5, 6, and 7 looked on the point of Santa Fe's hot 991 train (upper left) in California's Franklin Canyon in 1986, a sea change had taken place. Hundreds of SD60s like UP 6060 (right) in the Feather River Canyon in 1989 were to roam North American railroads.

Nestled in the Sierra Nevada foothills, away from the mainstream of Class I railroad happenings, the tiny Amador Central ran a simple, straightforward operation between Martel and Ione, California, hauling mostly wood chips from owner Georgia-Pacific's plant to an SP interchange. At one point, the tiny carrier hauled four cars of fine sawdust to Georgia-Pacific each week for use in making premium particleboard at the mill. Power for the operation was a Baldwin. Engine No. 9 was an S12 switcher, built in 1951 and purchased by the Amador Central from Sharon Steel. In January 1974, No. 9 drops downgrade from Georgia-Pacific with four carloads of wood chips and six boxcars loaded with finished wood products. The engineer has to keep her speed down, due to the steep grade in spots and the light rail under his charge. In the late 1990s, Sierra Pacific Lumber bought all of Georgia-Pacific's holdings in the Martell area, including the railroad. The new owner shut down the mill and the railroad, since it was only interested in G-P's timber holdings. Recently, the railroad reopened under new ownership as the Amador Foothills Railroad, showing the ebb and flow of a shortline railroad's fortunes.

With the Central Valley shrouded in fog, Amador Central No. 9 crosses Highway 49, headed for Ione under blue skies in the Sierra foothills in January 1974.

Permanence. It's something that can't be taken for granted, especially in the world of railroading. Take the WP's mainline through Stockton, California. The fledgling railroad laid its tracks through this town at the crossroads of the Central Valley in the first decade of the twentieth century, and in August 1910, passenger trains began running in direct competition with the SP. Until it was acquired by the UP in 1982, the company passed through two bankruptcies and reorganizations, the Great Depression, and a hostile takeover attempt by the SP. Still, the WP endured. It was one of the first railroads in the country to order EMD's FT diesel-electrics for freight service. During World War II it saw freight and passenger traffic soar to the point that its single Salt Lake City–Oakland varnish, the *Exposition Flyer*, ran in as many as eight sections. To help keep the Feather River Canyon from becoming a bottleneck for the pounding war traffic, the railroad had installed Centralized Traffic Control, or CTC, between Oroville and Portola by June 1945. But when UP and SP merged in 1997, the WP's main through Stockton became superfluous, and two years later was removed. Thus something long seen as a fixture in Stockton disappeared as quickly as it had been installed. Crossing the Santa Fe diamonds, WP 2256 West will enter Stockton Yard after bringing a manifest from Salt Lake City.

WP 3531 West, a long manifest, splices downtown Stockton on a pleasant afternoon in May 1973. The track she's on is now gone, and this neighborhood lies underneath the Cross-town Freeway.

At times during its last decade of existence, SP was so strapped for power that it leased whatever units it could find, in whatever shape they might be. This was a tremendous drain on the company's precious resources, both from the costs of leasing and the constant need to nurse such units into working order. In 1994, GE and SP negotiated a financing package that allowed the carrier to take delivery of 279 AC4400CWs in 1995. With the 101 Dash 9s delivered a year earlier, they were a great boost to SP's ailing locomotive fleet; they were also the last new units SP would buy. Unlike the Dash 9s, which were assigned mainly to the railroad's Intermountain and Sunset Route lines, the ACs were in large part placed in service in the mountain passes of the Far West, such as Tehachapi, Donner, the Cascades, and across the Basin and Range of Nevada. Despite having alternating current traction motors, they were used not only on heavy coal drags, but also on a variety of other trains, such as manifests and autoracks. Roseville Yard became one of their major terminals, and they congregated on the ready tracks there and in its "Cape Canaveral" servicing facility. Here, a trio of ACs brings 11,000 tons of Utah coal down the Donner grade at Rocklin in May 1996.

On any one day, the AC4400CWs could be found in force on the "Hill," like this pair pulling an empty autorack train around the edge of the American River Canyon on a sunny afternoon in October 1995.

In May 1996, AC4400CWs 343 and 327, barely six months old, proudly wear the scarlet and gray as they pause between assignments at Roseville Yard at sunset.

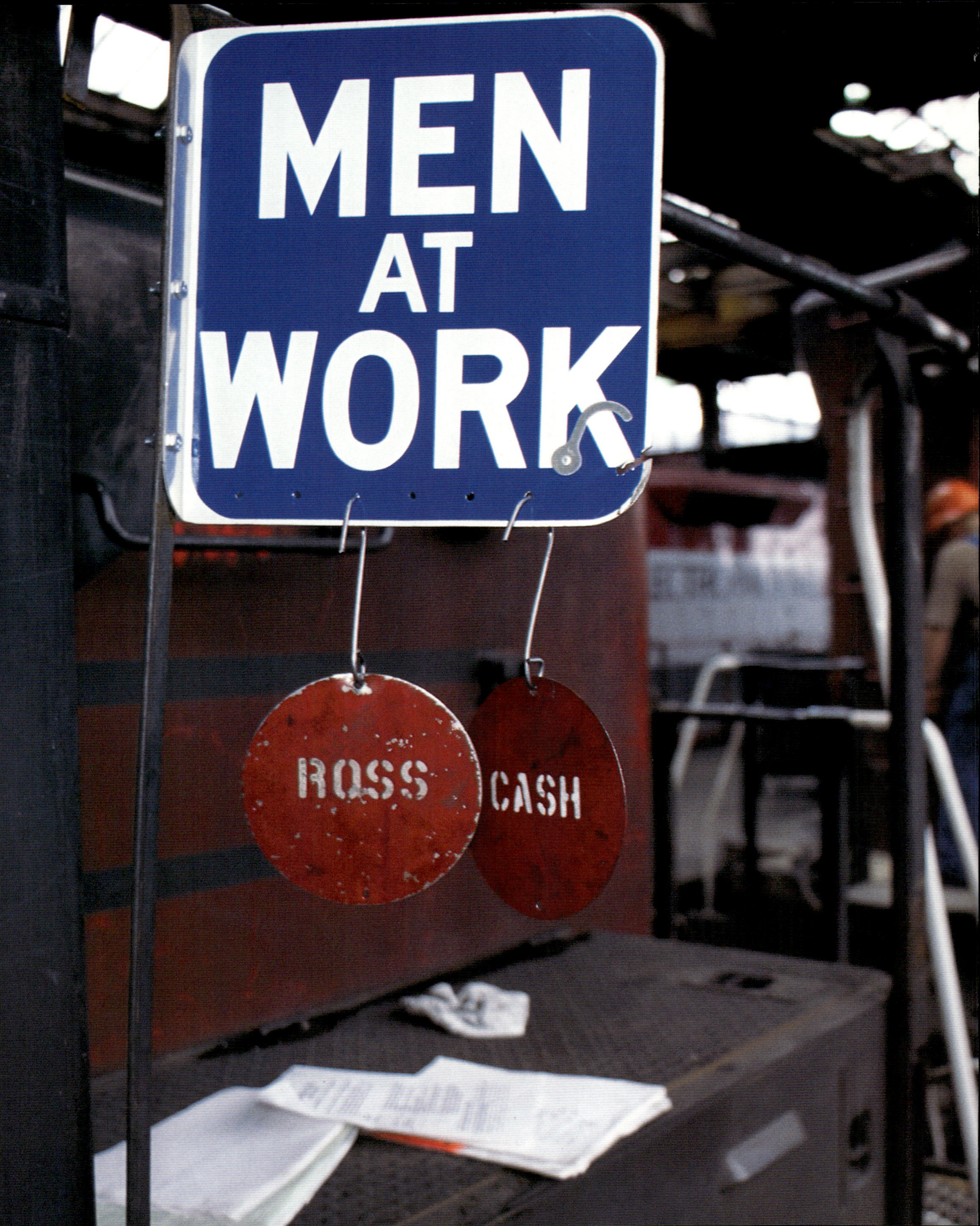
MEN
AT
WORK
ROSS
CASH

Chapter Three

RAILROADERS
at
WORK

$\mathcal{A}$t the beginning of the twentieth century, North American railroads employed veritable armies of people. They were major employers, and in many small towns the *only* employers, with virtually every extended family having one or more of its members on a railroad's payroll. Maintaining and moving trains over the road called for the intervention of people at almost every turn: telegraphers and tower operators; engine wipers; bridge, switch, and grade-crossing tenders; firemen and multiple brakemen; huge gangs of gandy dancers—the list goes on. Some jobs no longer exist, outmoded by the switch from steam to diesel or by the introduction of electronics or other improvements. Others still take their titles from that list, but their job descriptions are increasingly distinct from those of their counterparts from yesteryear.

People and the jobs they perform may not be the first things most people's minds conjure up when they think of railroads, but they're definitely the most important. People *are* the railroad! They're the real "motive power" that drives everything in the industry. Without them, locomotives idle and cars sit on countless yard tracks and sidings. Nothing moves. With them, the railroad and images of it come to life.

Something to consider: Just as the North American megamergers and acquisitions of the 1990s reflect the personalities involved—the amicability and ambition of management at BN and ATSF; the thirst for empire endemic in the culture at UP; Mike Haverty's and KCS's quest to outdo the big guys, personified in the highly leveraged Transportacion Ferroviaria Mexicana; and the brash determination of Norfolk Southern's bosses to get a piece of Conrail—so, too, railroading in the trenches mirrors the character of the people who make it happen.

As railroading in North America—the United States, Canada, and Mexico—has increased in capital intensity, people have become less and less an obvious part of the picture. Today an observer without a scanner could pace a train on a U.S. Class I railroad, for example, over its entire 300-mile run between crew changes without hearing or seeing a single railroad employee. In the days of steam or early diesels, such an impersonal trip would have been impossible. At certain intervals, men would have appeared atop tenders to refill them from a water tank, or hung out the side of a cab unit as another person, probably well known to locals, hooped up orders.

But are people really a less important factor in railroading today? Can capital and technology really diminish the importance of the human element? If the UP–SP debacle following their merger has shown anything, it's that when you don't know how to handle people, your enterprise suffers terribly. Unlike machines, people often do *not* perform best when they're centralized and insulated hundreds or even thousands of miles from the operating territory they're charged with managing in real time.

Compared to us eight-to-fivers, most railroaders in the operating department live quite a different life. Their schedule varies from day to day, they're away from home a lot, they work nights, and sometimes they vanish for weeks without a trace. I've had the pleasure of getting to know a couple of railroaders who work the UP out of Tucson. Jason is new to the industry, having hired on when he was barely 24. He works the extra board, and mostly catches assignments to El Paso that average 10-1/2 to 12 hours. Sometimes he's called west to Yuma or Phoenix, or down to Nogales on the United States–Mexico border. Kenny, on the other hand, is a veteran of 30 years who started with SP in 1969. Like Jason, he's a conductor and has never had much desire to move to the other side of the cab. The payoff for staying put? Tons of seniority. He's now a member of the "super pool," employees with enough time to catch only the choicest assignments, namely the "shooters" that usually get you the 313 miles to El Paso in a decent time. He lays over 12 to 14 hours and then catches another "hot symbol" coming west. Do that a few times a week and you pull down some good money and have a life that almost looks like a normal person's.

Jason observes, "With single track, if someone 'stubs their toe' out here, it clogs everything behind them." Kenny adds, "When you get the monsoon lightning storms, it can knock out the code lines, and then you have to flag past signals. It really slows things down." Rumor has it UP wants to run 80 trains a day on the Sunset Route, but that's really pushing it on a mostly single-track railroad. You spend a lot of time in sidings or waiting to get into El Paso, where the railroad complex wasn't designed for even the 30 to 40 trains it sees today.

One of the most amazing aspects of North American railroading is the amount of power and weight one person can control. A typical quartet of SD40-2s weighs in at approximately 720 tons, while the train it pulls may weigh upward of 10,000 tons. The man or woman at the throttle has mastery over that enormous mass. Given the amount of weight a human being can lift or push unassisted, which we usually express in hundreds of pounds or kilograms, at most, those are incredible figures. As a tool, the locomotive can be viewed as a mere extension of the engineer,

PREVIOUS PAGES: While two Southern Pacific employees prepare to work on an SD45's prime mover in the next bay, employees Ross and Cash are busy in this bay replacing power assemblies. In EMD engines, the piston, cylinder, injector, and valves come in a unit called a "power assembly," or simply "assembly." SP's Roseville Shops are a buzz of activity this afternoon in December 1996, with much coming and going of men and machines.

allowing him or her to leverage experience and training to an astronomical degree. Human strength is no longer a factor, being outstripped by combustion and weight on a scale large enough to be heard for miles. What's really mind-boggling is that, even at speed, the engineer is still in control. The fact that that control is somewhat tenuous only increases the drama.

Doubtless, 720 tons of locomotives and 10,000 tons of train cruising along a perfectly flat profile at 70 miles per hour on straight, smooth rails is a tremendous mass. If an unsuspecting child crawls onto the right-of-way or an impatient motorist drives around flashing crossing gates in front of this rolling monster, the engineer suddenly becomes painfully helpless. Throw in momentum, and you increase the anxiety tenfold. Tilt the profile so the railroad loses, say, 106 feet per mile, a 2.0 percent downhill grade, and that monster tries to pick up more speed with every turn of the wheels, making it even more difficult to stop. Were you sitting next to the engineer, you would feel the heat of the moment. Training and experience only count for so much with odds like this. Here lies much of the true and largely unappreciated drama of North American railroading: the highly accessible mainlines across our continent, opening the engineer and his companions to untold anxiety and risks.

Then there's the other side of railroading: in the shops, fueling facilities, and yards. When you step into a locomotive repair facility like UP's Burnham Shops in Denver, you know instantly you've entered a different world. The scale of machinery and parts is massive, much larger than the corresponding automotive facilities you may have frequented. The work is heavy. Everyone in the building wears a hard hat and steel-toed shoes, and a goodly number sport grease-stained overalls and dark, callused hands. The ceiling is high and the walls far apart, and the sounds of pounding and grinding ring across the concrete floor. Acrid smoke and blue haze float over scattered portions of the building's interior, tipping you off to the welding, cutting, and grinding that are creating them, while eerie, cold light from an arc welder casts bright shadows around certain workstations. Contrasting with the generally Spartan and even gloomy ambiance the giant shop exudes, laughter echoes from over here, jovial bantering from over there. The employees here working this shift seem to get along well and like what they do.

A seasoned locomotive shop workman is a pleasure to watch. He knows the all-important nuances of his craft in a way that only comes with time and experience. You can see it on his face when he flips up the shield protecting his eyes and face to inspect his work. From grinding a main-bearing A-frame to precise tolerances or carefully welding a tiny-but-significant crack in a damaged crankcase, to rebuilding an engine from the ground up, skilled labor daily proves itself not only a precious commodity, but a thing of beauty to watch.

The invention of the electric light has allowed railroads to continue their work unabated after sundown, and the focus of their nighttime bustle is the yard. Merchandise continues to be loaded in boxcars, trailers and containers are lifted onto platforms, and cars are blocked with others going to the same destination and dispatched at all hours. Every night, thousands of kilowatt-hours of electricity flow through utility meters and into powerful bulbs suspended atop giant lighting standards and poles. Power for refueling, brake shoe change-outs, running inspections, and the like runs through the engine facility. The tracks in big-time locomotive facilities are elevated slightly so mechanical folks can get a good look at the underside as well as at the upper portions of running gear without crouching too much. To inspect and repair locomotives on the night shift, you need lots of artificial light, not only overhead, but also shining from the side and underneath.

Thus, the pace of railroad work pulsates across the continent. Trains arrive and depart from yards and stations, while locomotives are serviced, repaired, and overhauled. Railcars are refurbished and rebuilt, sometimes to carry loads different from those for which they were called into service. Behind all this activity is the mind and muscle of people.

In August 1972, a Milwaukee Road track inspector waits patiently in a spur track for 2060 East to pass before he comes out onto the main to follow it. His job here just east of the summit of Pipestone Pass, Montana, is, among other things, to ensure that no fires started by sparks from the diesel locomotives get out of hand.

On a sunny afternoon in July 1973 at Willbridge, Oregon, a Burlington Northern switch crew is busy shunting cars with an ex–Spokane, Portland & Seattle Alco RS3. Once the crew has finished sorting cars here on the Portland side of the Columbia River, they'll head back to Vancouver, Washington, with a string of wood-chip cars and boxcars across the big double-track bridge that connects Oregon and Washington.

The BN operator at Vancouver, Washington, hoops up orders to a Milwaukee Road engineer on a freight headed for Tacoma in July 1973. Before the advent of widespread radio communication on North American railroads, train orders were a common way to transfer track authority. As radio came into common use in non-CTC territory, track warrants transmitted directly from dispatcher to train crews became the standard vehicle for transferring track authority, and thus operators were no longer needed.

On a calm evening in August 1972, the crew of a Milwaukee Road westbound has been waiting a couple hours for a train headed east. Now that it has passed, the "Dead Freight" is easing out of East Portal, Montana. The engineer has his two Little Joes creeping toward the long bore through the Bitterroot Mountains, as his brakeman prepares to mount the cab.

Craning his neck so as to see the brakeman on the ground and at the same time control the movements of Little Joe E-79, a Milwaukee Road engineer switches the small yard at Avery, Idaho, in July 1973. Obviously, switching with a Little Joe is not optimal, but as with so many other aspects of its operations, the Milwaukee Road, "America's Resourceful Railroad," made due with what was available this morning.

Milwaukee Road 3010 East, with a block of reefers in the front of its consist, pulls up to the depot at Avery, Idaho, in July 1973. A brakeman stands ready to couple on Little Joe E-79 to help the train over the Bitterroots. "In 1958–59," according to Noel Holley, a Milwaukee Road historian, "the Little Joes were modified to MU [multiple unit] with diesels by mounting a small diesel throttle next to the electric throttle and connecting it to the electric throttle with levers." Retired Milwaukee railroader Darrel Dewald states that Laurence Wylie, chief electrical engineer of the railroad for many years, came up with the idea. "In 1958, two years *after* his retirement, he introduced what came to be known as the 'Wylie Controller.' The concept was simple: a small, cab-mounted box that allowed electric engines to operate in multiple with diesel units by permitting diesel-electric throttles to be set proportionately with those of the 'straight' electric units. A removable link-pin permitted the engineer to control either type of power independently."

On a typical summer day in Butte, Montana, the engineer of helper engine E-45 walks over to have a chat with the crew of Milwaukee Road 3022 East, which he'll be assisting over Pipestone Pass. It's August 1973, and using the 55-year-old "boxcabs" to help trains east out of Butte is still routine. In a few minutes, the engineer will climb into the cab of the venerable GE and with a slight "hum" from his locomotive will ease it toward the coupler of the lead SD40-2.

Railroaders at Work 67

It's late in the day, and a Western Pacific crew is busy switching a string of Union Pacific cars at the west end of Stockton Yard. On this clear day in May 1973, the switch crew's head brakeman is using a red cloth to signal to the brakeman uncoupling cars. WP purchased engine No. 581, a Baldwin VO-1000 with 60,000 pounds of tractive effort, in September 1945, when steam power still ruled the railroad.

Newly painted Sacramento Northern EMD NW2u 607 brings a long string of cars just in from the Pacific Northwest on a transfer run to the Santa Fe interchange in Stockton, California, in May 1973. Something appears to be amiss with 607's prime mover, as evidenced by the plume of white smoke spewing from the switcher's exhaust stack. A Santa Fe Alco switcher will retrieve the cars from the interchange tracks, and they'll be switched into a train bound for the Los Angeles Basin.

In March 1988, the head brakeman on SP's Shell Unit Oil Train heads back up to the lead locomotives after trying to locate the problem that's caused the train to dump its air. After about an hour of searching, the problem is finally found, and the swing helper's four EMDs roar to life. The lead engineer notches out the throttle relatively quickly, since the slack is already taken out in this uphill train.

Two FM H-12-44s switch SP's Third and Townsend Street Station in San Francisco early on a Saturday morning in January 1974. The 2355's crew is discussing what the next move will be, while the 2372's crew waits patiently for the next commuter train from San Jose. Once the crews have taken all of the commuter trains' Harriman suburban coaches and bilevels to the coach yard, they'll tie their engines up at the Seventh Street engine facility.

Northwestern Pacific train crews compare notes and exchange trains at Windsor, California, in 1999. One crew brought a consist down from Willits, and the other a train up from Schelleville. The crew of 4324 South brought a train over Ridge Hill, and thus required three SD9s to do the job.

70   Chapter 3

A brakeman checks out equipment on the lead SD9 of an NWP passenger special headed for Willits. No. 4324 North is holding the mainline here at Hopland, California, waiting to meet 4305 South. The 4324's conductor is on the ground in front of the train making sure that none of the many passengers gets too near the siding. In a few minutes, the 4305 will slide by, and with two blasts from his horn, the 4324's engineer will highball.

Railroaders at Work 71

Workers at SP's Roseville Shops change out a governor in SD7 1521 in November 1996. Sister 1518 was EMD's first six-axle road switcher, having started life as EMD Demonstrator No. 990, and saw many years of service holding down switching duties at SP's Roseville Yard.

Messieurs Ross and Cash, veterans of many an engine rebuilding, prepare to insert new assemblies into an SD45 at SP's Roseville Shops. Old assemblies appear dark, while new ones are a silver color. Once they've positioned an assembly, they lock it into position using a giant air wrench.

The Denver & Rio Grande Western's Burnham Shops in Denver are alive with activity on this evening in March 1997. At the southwest corner of the shop building, a couple of workers are busy reassembling ex-SP EMD SD40T-2 8364. The Tunnel Motor has seen over a million miles of use, and is likely to see at least that many more after being rebuilt.

Railroaders at Work

In January 2002, a UP signal maintainer puts new wayside signals into operating position as a tamper puts the finishing touches on the new, second mainline track at Luzena, Arizona. Later on this Saturday, UP will place in service this new stretch of double-track mainline between here and Raso, Arizona.

An SP maintenance-of-way gang replaces ties on the mainline at Marcel, California, in Tehachapi Pass in March 1992. After the new ties are inserted, a tamper goes over the line to ensure the heavy welded rail is properly supported by ballast and that it is perfectly in gauge and aligned.

As light fails on a full day of work in November 1996, a BNSF employee uses a rail cutter to saw off the end of a piece of rail so that it will fit with rail that's already been laid and secured to concrete ties. Amtrak California paid the $31 million bill for this installation of double track between Oakley and Bixler, California, that allows it to run more *San Joaquins* on this ex–Santa Fe route between the Bay Area and Bakersfield.

With the giant mounds of Ray Mine as a backdrop, Copper Basin Railway train OT-1, trailing 60 loaded ore hoppers, makes its way slowly through Ray Junction, where the line to Florence splits off from the line into the mine. Once at the dumper in Hayden, OT-1's engineer will pull the first two thirds of the train through, and then run around it to push the remaining third through.

Early on a summer morning in 1999, a Copper Basin Railway crew and personnel from Mountain States Contractors load a culvert on a flatcar at Hayden, Arizona. During the night, a trestle burned in Florence, severing the railroad's link with the UP at Magma. The railroad will replace the trestle with the culvert, packing unopened bags of concrete around it and then wetting them down to form an erosion-proof, low-cost retaining wall.

Attitude is everything on the Copper Basin, as attested by the slogan on the side of one of the small carrier's gray-and-copper-colored locomotives.

77

RIGHT: Buffing a wax coat that's been applied to Santa Fe EMD SD75M 234, a BNSF employee prepares it and a sister unit at the Barstow LMIT for a special train they'll pull the following day to the 1996 Super Bowl.

At BNSF's Barstow, California, Locomotive Maintenance and Inspection Terminal (LMIT), an employee tops off the fuel tank of an ex–Santa Fe warbonnet GE. The Barstow LMIT is BNSF's nerve center for all of its California operations.

78   Chapter 3

In September 1997, BNSF 726 West roars through the little town of Knightsen, California, on its way to Richmond. A group of the town's inhabitants, many of whom are farmers and ranchers, have recently constructed this sign to show their pride in their community's heritage.

79

In the rugged mountains of the Mexican state of Nayarit, Ferrocarriles del Pacifico train No. 1, the northbound *El Costeño*, meets a freight and No. 4, a second-class passenger train headed for Guadalajara in June 1978. *El Costeño's* consist includes several Pullmans from north of the border, along with Japanese-made, air-conditioned coaches.

As a venerable Alco FA makes its way through FCP's Guadalajara engine facility, an employee washes one of the railroad's Montreal Locomotive Works M420TRs. Always a purchaser exclusively of four-cycle diesel power, FCP was one of the last North American havens of big Alcos and MLWs. The railroad continued buying four-stroke power, later from GE, to keep its fleet standardized for its mechanical forces.

80 *Chapter 3*

Railroaders at Work   81

With a BN hostler in the cab and two more working the turntable at Interbay Yard in Seattle, an ex-CB&Q EMD E8 is readied in August 1972 for its next assignment on a passenger train south to Portland. The big E-unit will eventually be reassigned to the railroad's commuter service in Chicago.

On a warm summer afternoon in August 1972, EMD DDA40X 6941 is run through UP's wash rack in Portland, Oregon. Later in the afternoon, the big double-diesel will lead an eastbound up the Columbia River Gorge.

Pulling on a cord that allows sand to pass through the hose he has inserted into BN 4264's rear sand port, a WP employee continues down the line of ex-SP&S Alcos he's working on this afternoon in May 1972 at the railroad's Stockton Yard.

Railroaders at Work 83

With Stockton Tower's operator looking on, Amtrak 426 West trundles through the SP diamonds on a spring afternoon in April 1974. In a half-mile, the train from Bakersfield will stop at the beautiful ex–Santa Fe depot, where many patrons will off-board to ride an Amtrak bus to Sacramento.

Two ex-SP EMD FP7s hold down an eastbound Amtrak *San Joaquin* at Merced, California, in March 1974. With typical puffy white clouds floating over the Central Valley, a container-on-flatcar (COFC) freight headed for Richmond passes the aging, boiler-equipped cab units, its conductor and rear brakeman giving a hearty hello to the passenger train's crew. When the *San Joaquins* ran with an FP7, mechanical forces in Oakland would usually assign two such units to a train in case one of the units' steam boilers failed.

Brand-new UP EMD SD70M 5054 holds on No. 2 track just east of Prince Road in Tucson, Arizona, with a westbound stack train, as its conductor gives a roll-by to an opposing movement. No doubt 5054's crew appreciates the amenities in the new diesel's cab, including a refrigerator that actually works! It is October 2002, and the locomotive is making its maiden voyage to the West Coast.

A Rentzenberger van has just dropped off the crew for UP 4462 West at Stockham in Tucson, Arizona, on a chilly night in January 2002. The railroad has held all westbound trains here until nightfall due to track work to the west. One of several westbounds is now passing the 4462, and when it clears, the engineer will let the dispatcher know he's ready to depart.

Railroaders at Work   87

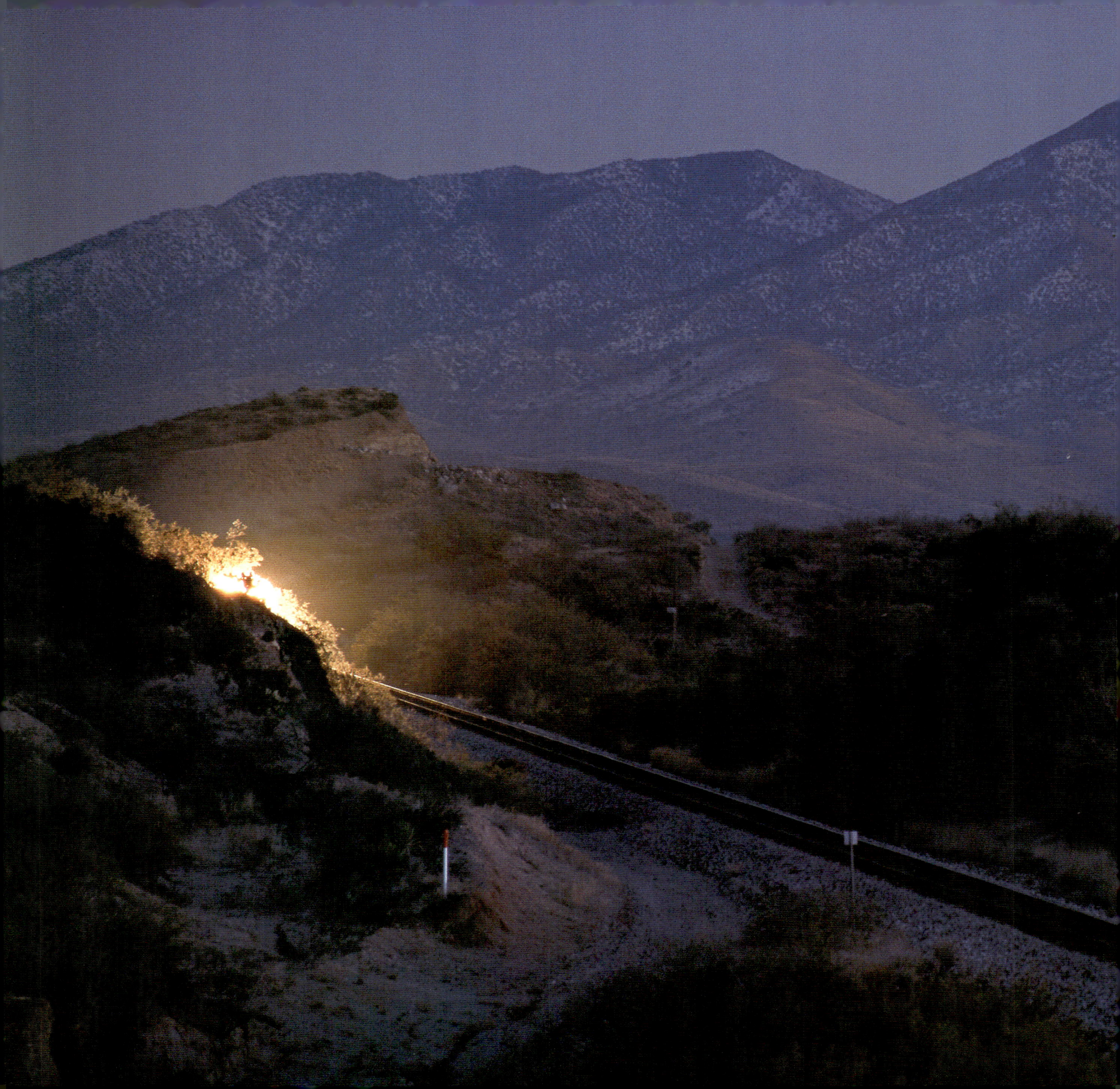

Chapter Four

The RAILROAD NEVER SLEEPS

*B*ecause railroading in North America entails the transport of goods over long distances, it is an industry that runs around the clock. In the highly integrated economy of the United States—and to an increasing degree in the economies of Canada and Mexico—production and distribution depends on the timely delivery of shipments transported by rail. In the western regions of the continent, across the many mountain ranges, vast deserts, and long valleys, and along the winding rivers, the distance between traffic centers is great. Goods often take days to arrive at their destination, and that means that some train crews work in daylight, and others under cover of darkness. Switch crews in the yards continue to sort cars and make up new trains, and welders and workmen in the shops get locomotives back into shape for their next assignments—at all times of the day and night.

In the darkness, wayside signals guide and control the movement of trains. Signals define much of the character of nighttime railroading. During daylight, their *aspects*—the information they display—appear low-key, but in the dark they become luminescent emerald, topaz, and ruby-red jewels. Observing railroad operations at nighttime is a palpably different animal from its diurnal counterpart. Not only do signals bounce their liquid colors off the railhead, but locomotive headlights become bright infernos that, if you're in the right location, shine across 40, 50, and even 60 miles of terrain, announcing a train's approach an hour or more ahead of time. It's no wonder engineers dim their headlights when they meet another train; doing so entails more than common courtesy. Once their head-ends pass, the lights are switched back on to scan for defects, shifted loads, and unauthorized riders.

In territory where automatic block signals reign, governing occupancy in predetermined stretches of track, dispatchers usually control train movements via radio-transmitted track warrants. In the old days, such orders were relayed to local operators who hooped them up to train crews as "flimsies." In Centralized Traffic Control (CTC) territories, dispatchers transfer track authority via signal indications. Think of it: With the push of a tiny button, a dispatcher can clear a path for a 7,000-ton train hundreds of miles from where she sits. What power! The path becomes her "footprint," a string of glistening green pearls that beckons grateful crewmen onward. If and when the time comes that Class I dispatchers use global positioning systems instead of wayside signals to control their trains, it will mark a definite diminution to the character and color of nighttime railroading.

One account of railroading at night comes from ex–Milwaukee Road employee Darrel Dewald, who shares the following account regarding the fireworks that the electrification in Idaho and Montana could provide under the right conditions:

> Some years ago on a cold, moonless night, a train and engine crew were called in Alberton, Montana, for a trip to Avery, Idaho. I was a member of the crew, working as the head-end brakeman with engineer Adam Gratz. I am not now, at this late date, sure just who was the conductor or the rear brakeman. At that point in time the fireman position had already been eliminated.
>
> We departed Alberton with somewhere around 4,300 tons, with an engine consist of a Little Joe with two diesels controlled from the Joe through the "Wylie Controller." We did have some frost on the trolley leaving Alberton, but nothing really unusual. When we departed St. Regis, Montana, we began picking up more frost on the trolley wire, and the electric arc from the pantograph began to be quite steady. As we arrived at Foraker, the frost was real heavy and the arc was just about continuous. If one had ever noticed the brightness of an arc welder, just think of this being about tenfold brighter! The arc lit up both sides of the canyon walls to make it look just like daylight. It would light up the area and then drop back to the dark of night, and then arc again. This was very hard on the eyes, as one can imagine. You had to close your eyes or hold your head down. I tried sunglasses, but that was not much help, and it was bad when the arc stopped—you couldn't see because of the darkness. Adam and I would take turns resting our eyes by closing them as we proceeded up the track.
>
> The MG (motor-generator) sets would even make a winding-down sound as we hit the heavy frost. Adam was running with both "pans" up to help prevent this from happening. I don't remember just how long we had this frost condition, but it seemed like a long time.
>
> I often wonder what those traveling along in their cars thought when they were hit with this extremely bright electrical flash that was more or less continuous. It had to be very hard on them driving into such a bright light. It was a good thing there were not many automobiles at that time of the night.
>
> This arcing could be very hard on the pantograph shoes, and could, in fact, burn right through them. Luckily, we didn't have that happen on this trip.

Another tale of round-the-clock railroading comes from William Franckey, who worked the Burlington Northern out of Chicago:

> Night after night on the Fox River job out of Cicero, ordered at 11:40 P.M., we would take six SDs off the pit to our train for departure to Aurora, on the branch to Wedron, Ottawa, Streator, and [then] return—30, 40, 50 nights in a row, then a night or two off, then another 40 trips. I worked the job close to 70 straight nights, took a trip off and worked it again for 40 trips before another night off.

PREVIOUS PAGES: As night settles over Arizona's Whetstone Mountains on December 14, 2001, the headlight of an approaching Union Pacific freight headed for Tucson illuminates the vegetation along No. 1 track. The train, the Northline Local, is returning from Lordsburg, New Mexico, where this morning the train's crew gathered various loaded cars. Tonight, the crewmembers will sleep in a warm, familiar bed, not something they get to enjoy every night.

The regular engineer, E.E. Eversoll, said to me one night, "You don't lay off much, do you?" Quite a compliment, as he had a reputation for working it regular himself. This was the highest paying job on the BN system, or so I was told. Night after night with six SD7s and 9s.

We began to notice something strange about these locomotives. Certain nights, once in a while, we would get a GP40 at one end of the consist, so upon reaching Streator, we would switch ends and start the run back to Chicago. It would only take a couple of nights before we started to notice our kidneys getting sore. I was in my early twenties and felt it, so I know everyone did. The four-wheel trucks of a GP40 would not ride as well as the six-wheel trucks of our regular locomotives. It took working the job for extended periods before one would start to put two and two together.

Dave Stanley, Winterail founder and an engineer for UP who's logged many a mile in California's Feather River Canyon, draws a comparison between EMD's products and those of its archrival, General Electric. "Although the GEs are slower and tend to shut themselves down somewhat [due to amperage limits] at about 63 miles per hour," Stanley says, "they still out-pull an EMD at slower speeds. The GEs don't shut down, per se; they just drop their amps to about 100 and can't make max speed. EMDs will attain top speed faster [than GEs] on level track."

Stanley also says that he prefers SD40-2s to EMD's newer products. "They tend to be a bit more reliable despite their age. I've had just as many SD60s act up as I have the older units. SD40-2s tend to pull better on light grades, and rarely slip. SD60s tend to be quieter, but not much."

Ted Benson and I can attest to Stanley's observation that EMDs attain track speed quickly. On a summer evening in 1984 at the old crew office in Oroville, California, we, along with Dave Styffe, Lynn Powell, and Gary Holmes, witnessed UP's *Overland Mail West* leave town with a vengeance. The power for the moderate-sized pig train was DDA40X No. 6908 and two SD40-2s. After changing crews in the stillness of dusk, the engineer was given a "high green" and wasted no time in responding. By the time the rear car passed us, the *OMW* had created a wind powerful enough to throw generous amounts of dust into the air and dishevel our hair and clothing as though we were standing in a gale. That was one of the most impressive displays of acceleration I've ever witnessed on a Class I railroad, and it drove home the unquestioned ability of EMD's "Dash 2" technology to get a train out of town fast.

Doug Harrop, longtime engineer on the SP and now with the UP in Nevada, relates a nighttime experience involving the new, high-tech locomotives Class I railroads are now using:

We came off Montello Hill one night and heard on the radio a young engineer with a problem at Pigeon, 25 miles to the east. A train had been parked there for days; this was during the UP service crisis in 1998. Finally, three SD9043MACs had been set out for the train and the young engineer could not get the lead unit to communicate with "Fred" on the rear of the train. It had been determined by another passing train that Fred was working, so the problem was on the engine, probably the computer.

The second and third units could not be moved up because of a frozen angle cock, so for the next hour and a half we listened to Mr. Goodwrench in Omaha solve the problem. He explained how to dismantle parts of the "Rockwell Box" [computer] in the nose of the lead unit and replace them with similar parts from the second unit. The engineer followed instructions, and after a very long time—we were now 40 miles east of Pigeon—the problem was fixed. At one point my conductor said to me, "I wouldn't do that—I couldn't do that!" I agreed. We were both in our late fifties.

Nowadays, as an old engineer, you receive no training in how to operate new power. No booklets, no brochures, nothing. You climb on the new engine, sit down, try to figure it out, and hope for the best. The new, young breed of engineer will get along just fine with the highly technical new power. But they will never experience the thrills associated with the old locomotives.

And so it goes. The lure of railroading is in part due to the character of its nighttime operations. At sunset and dusk, trains disappear into the blackness that forms the canvas for their activities. Crossing gates, wayside signals, a dispatcher giving instructions, a brakeman with a lantern—all are players on that canvas—because the railroad never sleeps.

At dusk in July 1972, the engineer of Southern Pacific 4008 West, a local, switches cars at Lathrop, California, where the line to Tracy and the coast splits off from the line to Fresno and Tehachapi. The engineer peers back out the Alco RS32's window to see what his brakeman is doing in the failing light.

92 Chapter 4

In May 1984, the round-end observation on the World's Fair special *Daylight* train from Portland, Oregon, to New Orleans sits in quietude at SP's coach yard in San Francisco.

An engineer and his conductor sit comfortably in the cab of SP EMD SD40T-2 8284 as the big Tunnel Motor and four mates scream slowly uphill out of Indio, California, with a train of iron ore from Kaiser Steel's Eagle Mountain Mine. The train is bound for Fontana on the other side of Beaumont Hill in May 1983, and it will be well into morning before the crew is relieved at West Colton.

The Railroad Never Sleeps   93

Sunlight is starting to illuminate the eastern sky as Santa Fe 5947 East approaches Ilmon in Tehachapi Pass. The lead unit began life in Santa Fe's red and silver warbonnet paint, but was subsequently painted into the carrier's freight scheme after Amtrak took over virtually all U.S. passenger service in May 1971. Two-thirds of the way back in the manifest, an SD26 and a pair of SD24s that were cut in at Edison before daybreak help lift the train up the increasing gradient.

94   Chapter 4

A Santa Fe intermodal train headed for Chicago approaches Stockton Tower under a fiery show at sunset in February 1991. The tower operator is protecting the train's movement through his "plant" via signals he controls on both the SP and ex–Western Pacific mainlines.

Under monsoon skies that are becoming increasingly forbidding in August 2002, a hot UP Z train blasts over Rillito's west switch. By the time the crew steps off at Tucson in 20 minutes, the sky will be pitch black.

UP 657 East climbs toward Estrella on the Sunset Route as light fades in March 1998. The long merchandise train has been climbing since Gila Bend, and the sounds from its locomotives have been floating over the cacti and palo verdes since well before it came into view.

In March 2002, three brand-new UP "flag" EMD SD70Ms glisten at dusk as a Rentzenberger van delivers a crew for the train parked at Stockham in Tucson. In 10 minutes, the engineer will blow his horn to alert motorists crossing the tracks on Sunset Road and will begin his nighttime crossing of the Sonoran Desert.

Two eastbound UP stack trains wait shy of Rillito, Arizona, for a crew to walk back from a westbound they've just parked in the siding to an empty eastbound autorack sitting on the mainline. The autorack's crew "died" here on this warm evening in June 2002, necessitating the juggling of crews that now has traffic backed up for miles in both directions.

UP 9773 streaks westward on the Sunset Route at dusk near Red Rock, Arizona, on September 1, 2001. Luckily for the crew, the manifest has been making good time since going into the siding at Rillito for a meet with a merchandise train out of Phoenix. Engine No. 9773 is one of the first GE Dash 9s to receive the UP's wings on its nose and the lightning stripe on its flanks. Crews like the Dash 9s because they ride and pull well.

A couple of Milwaukee Road brakemen called for 8 P.M. on an eastbound freight chat in the yard at Avery, Idaho, on the evening of July 31, 1973. The power for their train rests quietly in the background: a couple of Little Joes and an EMD GP9 up front, and an ancient boxcab for swing helper. The brakemen will work the train over St. Paul Pass and be relieved at Alberton, Montana.

On a cool night in July 1973, Milwaukee Road boxcab E-29 sits outside the well-illuminated locomotive shed at Avery, Idaho. The source of the electricity lighting the shed is the same that courses through the trolley wire overhead, although the trolley wire receives power as 3,000-volt DC, while the lights receive it as 120-volt AC. According to Noel Holley, "each A-B set" of boxcabs "cost as much as several steam locomotives. The Milwaukee began combining units into three-unit A-C-B sets during the 1930s, and into A-D-C-B sets in the 1950s." To sum up their performance, Noel says, "The GE motors were simple, rugged, and reliable."

UP's Stockton engine facility is busy in February 1996 as a hostler moves a string of ex–Chicago & North Western GE Dash 9s to another track. In the foreground is the "pit," where mechanical forces can inspect the underbelly of locomotives.

At dusk, the engineer of Northwestern Pacific 3844 South and an old friend chat in Healdsburg, California. On this crystal-clear evening in October 1996, the passenger special will tie up here after completing a round trip to Willits.

Canadian National's *Supercontinental* passenger train pauses at Kamloops, British Columbia, behind FP9 6509 in August 1972. In a few minutes, a new crew will step aboard and disappear into the night toward Jasper National Park. CN transferred FP9 6509 to Via Rail Canada in 1978.

On the evening of December 19, 1995, SP's "Cape Canaveral" engine facility in Roseville, California, is alive with activity. A mechanic (above) checks out several systems on aging SD9 4402 while two SD70Ms idle away before being refueled and sanded. Later, Sue Browning and Robert Verascal (upper right) compare notes while sanding and refueling a pair of GE AC4400CWs. Earlier in the evening, a veteran diesel mechanic (right) shows a novice how to replace the brake shoes quickly and properly on a string of EMD locomotives.

105

106 *Chapter 4*

The headlight on the lead EMD SD70M of a long UP stack train illuminates the metallic surfaces of the power and cars of a westbound unit grain train parked at Wilmot Road in Tucson. Although the grain train is not a high-priority movement, in a few hours she'll get a fresh crew to take her to Yuma, Arizona. The crew of the stack train is part of the "super pool" that runs trains exclusively between Tucson and El Paso, Texas, with no drags that terminate in Lordsburg, New Mexico.

Normally, monsoon storms that hit Tucson either come up from the south or build up over the Santa Catalina Mountains immediately north of the city, but on this evening of August 16, 2001, a big cell has moved in from the east. Shortly after dark at Rita Road on the eastern edge of the city limits, a beautiful sunset transforms into a menacing beast spewing lightning and whipping up dust right on top of UP's double-track Sunset Route mainline.

The Railroad Never Sleeps   107

The headlight of a westbound Santa Fe intermodal train at Orwood, California, beams across the giant water pipes of East Bay Municipal Utility District. It's October 21, 1991, and the day prior the spectacular Oakland Hills Fire, which destroyed hundreds of homes, filled the whole region with particulates from its dastardly work. It's a half-hour past sunset, and the sky has taken on an ominous red glow.

WP EMD F7A 920D sits in silence in front of the railroad's Stockton Shops on a cold night in January 1972. The venerable cab unit sustained mortal damage when a vandal threw a switch against her in the Feather River Canyon and an opposing train cut her face almost in two. A shop worker steam cleaning locomotive parts nearby creates a ghostly mist around the F. Her operating days are over.

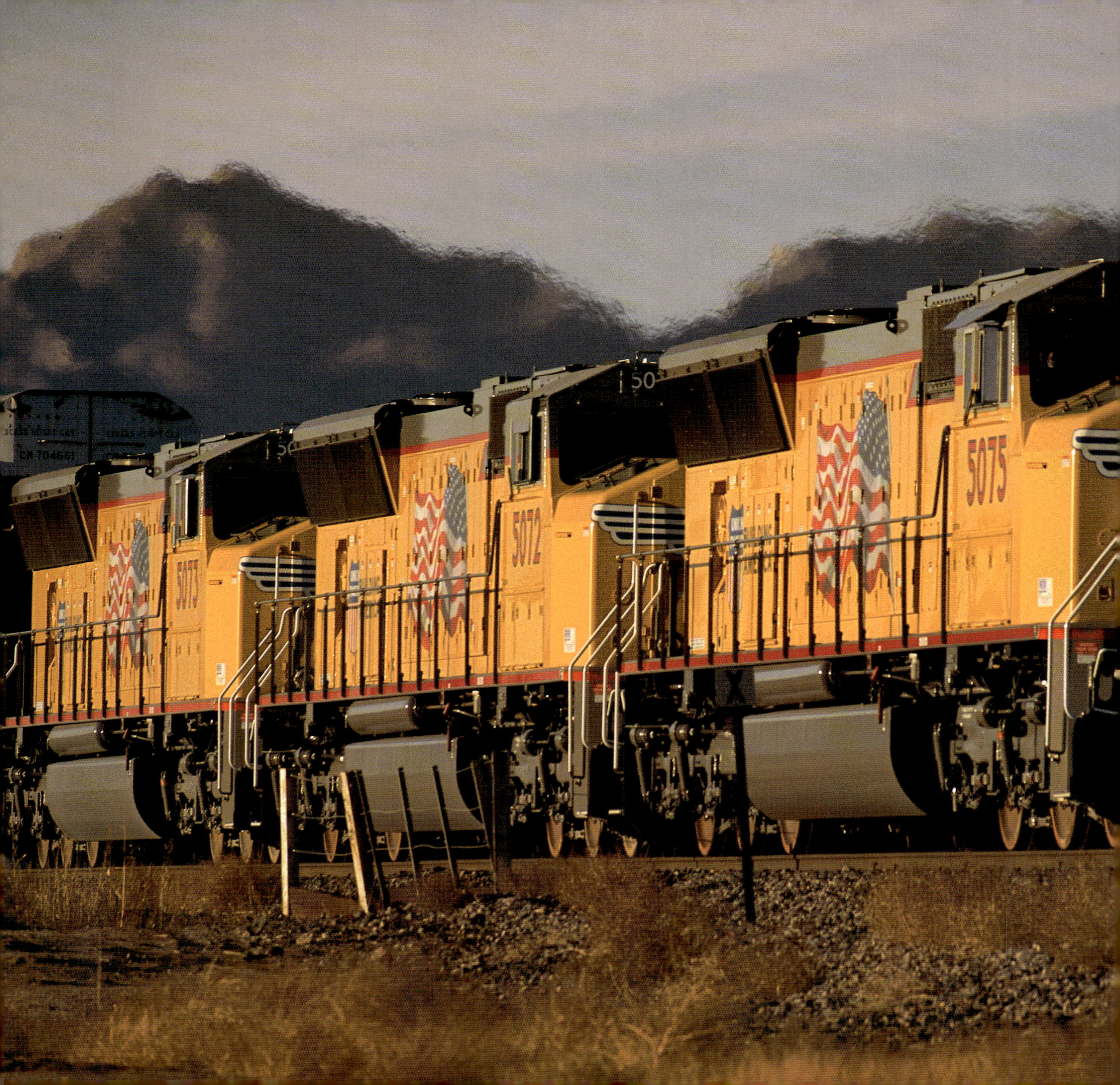
5073
5072
5075
CN 704661

Chapter Five

The EVOLUTION of a MACHINE

*A*s steam power reached the zenith of its development—as embodied in Lima "super power" locomotives pioneered in 1925 and typified by Southern Pacific's famous GS-4 Class passenger engines—diesel-electric locomotives were just coming into their own. According to Ben Coifman in *The Evolution of the Diesel Locomotive in the United States*, "In 1929, General Motors decided that there would probably be a large-scale market for diesel-powered locomotives in the near future; enough of a market to support a full production line. Immediately following the acquisition of EMC in 1930, General Motors shifted research and development efforts to the production of a diesel engine satisfactory for railcar and locomotive use.

"Both Winton in Cleveland and GM in Detroit worked on the development of a two-cycle engine. The other diesel locomotive builders had used four-cycle engines almost exclusively up to this point in time."

The cycles Coifman mentioned refer to the number of up and down strokes the piston makes in the cylinder. "General Motors decided that they could get a big jump in power by using a two-cycle engine design; however, the added power came at a price. A two-cycle engine will run hotter, experience more stress and have a lower power-to-stroke ratio than a four-cycle engine. At the time, fuel efficiency and engine life were not an issue," Coifman wrote, meaning such considerations were not first and foremost in the minds of the engine's designers. Rather, "matching the power of the steam engine was, and thus GM went with the two-cycle engine."

In 1933, Winton's engineers came out with their new prime mover, the W201A, available in 8-, 12-, and 16-cylinder versions. The W201A was a key to GM's later successes, since it served as the forerunner to the company's amazingly successful 567 powerplant. GM retained the EMC (Electro-Motive Corporation) name until the two companies merged in 1941, when it became the Electro-Motive Division of General Motors. GM remained the unquestioned leader in the field of diesel-electric locomotives until General Electric knocked it off its pedestal in 1993. Unlike GE, which has used four-cycle engines to power all of its diesel-electric offerings, starting with the U25B in 1959, EMD stuck with two-cycle prime movers until recently, when it developed the four-cycle "H" engine to power its 6,000-horsepower SD90MAC.

EMC introduced its 567 prime mover in March 1939, and first applied it in an E3 passenger locomotive. Shortly thereafter, it decided to tackle the freight locomotive market with its FT (for "Freight Twenty-seven hundred horsepower"). Over the next decade, Electro-Motive continued to upgrade its successful powerplant, which was rapidly knocking steam off the rails and grabbing the lion's share of the North American railroad market for GM.

A retired senior district leader from EMD's Service Department, Jack Wheelihan, brings more than 30 years of experience servicing the company's products to the table. To questions like, "What do you consider to be the strengths and weaknesses of particular EMD prime movers?" and "In what ways did the 645 improve on the 567?" Jack responds, "It must be understood that engine design progression and development take place over many, many years, resulting in small steps of continuous improvement. The 567C was an improvement over the B, which was, in turn, an improvement over the A.

"The design engineers must continually retain a balance between increasing stresses, cost-effective materials, manufacturability, maintainability, reliability, increasing fuel economy, and marketability."

To support Jack's point, note the following excerpt from an article that appeared in *The Brotherhood of Locomotive Firemen and Enginemen's Magazine* in 1954, featuring EMD's latest development:

A thousand horsepower increase in the propulsion power of a four-unit diesel freight locomotive is one of the improvements in a new line of ten types of railroad motive power announced by Electro-Motive Division of General Motors at La Grange, Illinois. The four-unit freight locomotive is increased from 6000 to 7000 horsepower. This is 1600 more than the horsepower rating of the first U.S. diesel freight locomotive brought out by Electro-Motive in 1940, reflecting technological advance in the locomotive field over the intervening period.

Most of the increases in ratings or in service life stem from the introduction of a new General Motors diesel engine, the 567-C series, upon which Electro-Motive engineers have been working for five years, and from a new traction motor which has been so greatly improved that it has [in the words of N. C. Dezendorf, General Motors vice president and EMD general manager] "made possible the elimination of arbitrary short-time ratings for all models and all gear ratios." The new models represent achievements from the series of development projects which are continuously carried on at Electro-Motive and which are aimed at improving performance and lengthening life of the locomotives and reducing maintenance costs. The new engine in the sixteen-cylinder version provides 1750 horsepower for propulsion. Its maximum rpm is 835 against 800 of its predecessor. Its size has not been increased. This sixteen-cylinder engine powers the F-9, FP-9, GP-9, and SD-9 models. The engine in all sizes (six, eight, twelve and sixteen cylinders) has an entirely new crankcase designed for longer service life. Frame members are

PREVIOUS PAGES: Fresh from the paint shop, three brand-new Union Pacific EMD SD70Ms have an 8,300-foot empty autorack train on their drawbar as they ascend the gentle eastward grade at Red Rock, Arizona, in November 2002. EMD equipped these units with its new split cooling system, required to meet EPA pollution standards that took effect in 2002; the flared radiators on the rear of the locomotives are the telltales. The SD70M represents EMD's state-of-the-art technology for direct-current locomotives.

heavier and the stress level of the entire crankcase is reduced, in spite of the higher horsepower output. The new traction motors, with the higher ratings of the new 567-C diesel engine, make it possible to haul more tons or haul the same tonnage faster.

In a two-cycle engine (more correctly called a "two-stroke-cycle" engine according to Wheelihan), the piston and its assisting machinery have to do all of the following in only two strokes: a) draw in fresh air and get rid of exhaust from the previous fuel explosion in the cylinder; b) compress the fresh air until it is superheated; and c) inject fuel into the cylinder, which immediately ignites and forces the cylinder downward. After the fuel ignites in the cylinder, pushing the piston downward, an exhaust valve at the top of the cylinder begins to open. When the connecting rod is at bottom dead center, the exhaust valve is fully open to allow expended gases to escape, and air intakes at the sides of the cylinder are completely uncovered to allow fresh air to fill it. This uncovering of the air intakes lasts for only a matter of milliseconds, so it's critical that a hefty amount of air enters the cylinder to achieve the requisite ignition of the diesel fuel. In normally aspirated EMD engines, a gear-driven "Roots" blower floods the cylinder with air at about 4 psi of pressure. In a turbocharged EMD prime mover, a thermal-reaction turbocharger, powered by the exhaust gases from the cylinder, forces fresh air into the cylinder at roughly four to five times the pressure as in normally aspirated engines. This supercharging of the air intake allows the same two-stroke engine to develop higher horsepower. As the piston begins its "up" stroke, it covers the air intakes, and the exhaust valve closes, sealing the cylinder for the oncoming compression. When the connecting rod is at top dead center, fuel enters the top of the cylinder through an injector and ignites, creating the explosion that powers the piston into its "down" stroke.

Max Ephraim Jr., who joined EMD in 1939 and led the teams of engineers that developed the 645 and later the 710, adds, "EMD had gone with the 567 originally in part because its engineers felt you could get more power out of a two-stroke engine compared to a four-stroke of the same size. As it turned out, this may have been true in theory, but did not materialize in practice. Both types of engines of similar size proved to have about the same power."

Regardless of whether or not the two-cycle prime mover actually delivered more power, Ephraim points out that "It's easier to build a four-cycle engine from scratch than a two-cycle. For example, timing on a two-cycle engine is more critical. It takes time to build a solid two-cycle engine." According to the retired chief engineer, other companies were quickly coming out with four-cycle engines from design to finished commercial product, some of which failed miserably.

Wheelihan qualifies Ephraim's statement regarding equal power for two- and four-cycle engines by adding, "The horsepower-to-weight ratio in a two-stroke engine is greater than that for a four-cycle engine. For example, the [four-cycle] 2,500-horsepower Cooper-Bessemer prime mover GE used to power its U25B weighed about 40,000 pounds more than the prime mover in EMD's GP35."

Ephraim recalls that in the 1960s it was fairly clear the railroads were looking for more horsepower. The 567 was maxed out at 2,500 horsepower, and Ephraim recalls the builder "could not increase the bore on the 567 any further without compromising it; that is, there was not enough crankcase area left to support a bigger bore." Ephraim added Electro-Motive also "wanted better reliability on all fronts, not just the prime mover itself—for example, in the electrical system—but the 'reliability program' really came later, as embodied in the Dash 2 line released in 1972."

An article appeared in the June 26, 1966, issue of *Railway Age* filled with the hype and promise that surrounded EMD's then new "1965-line" of locomotives. The piece featured Great Northern's purchase of eight SD45s, but spoke of the builder's other new offerings as well:

> *It* was not just a typical new locomotive which was displayed in Seattle last week. The big orange and olive unit, formally unveiled by the Great Northern for civic leaders and shippers at its West Coast terminal, is the most powerful single-engine

diesel-electric ever built. And GN was pointing out that it had just become the first railroad to acquire the 3,600-horsepower General Motors SD-45. A few weeks before the GN ceremony in the Puget Sound city, a pair of SD-45 demonstrator units pulled out of the Northern Pacific's Auburn, Washington, yard about 20 miles south of Seattle on what turned out to be a record-setting transcontinental run. This pair, aggregating 7,200 horsepower and bearing GM and Electro-Motive Division markings, headed up over the Cascade Mountains with a fast freight. Just four days—actually 96 hours and 40 minutes—later, the two SD-45s rolled to a stop in the Jersey City, New Jersey, yard of the Erie Lackawanna. In addition to the NP and E-L, the pair had traversed the Soo Line between St. Paul and Chicago, en route handling trains ranging from 3,000 to 6,500 tons. And they had averaged almost 35 miles per hour, including stops, a coast-to-coast timing which EMD believes to be a speed record for freight trains.

Since 1966, EMD and GE have produced several new models of "hood" and "wide-cab" diesel-electrics, and the slow, incremental evolution of the machine still continues. Regarding the three-piece windshields of EMD's early SD60Ms introduced in the 1980s, Dave Stanley, veteran engineer for the UP, comments, "The two-piece windshield does offer greater visibility over the older [three-piece] style. The three-piece windshield on early SD60Ms is lousy—it tends to throw false light reflections into your field of vision. I'm sure that's why they did away with it after the first orders of SD60Ms were delivered."

Al Krug, hogger for BN and now BNSF, expands on Dave's comments regarding the three-piece setup:

The first 50 or so SD60Ms came with the three-piece windshields. What a disaster! One gets the idea that no one at EMD ever sat in one of their own locomotives to see how things work out.

The three-piece windshields are vertical. The angle of the engineer's windshield is such that every light that is behind the locomotive off to the side on the conductor's side reflects off the engineer's windshield directly in the middle of his view of the track ahead. Imagine standing at the windshield directly in front of the engineer, but

In August 1972, ex–Southern Pacific GS-4 locomotive 4449 sits rusting away in Portland, Oregon. Several years before, the railroad had donated the steam engine to the city as a memento from the days when Lima superpower worked SP's passenger trains in and out of Portland.

Restored to her operating glory by Doyle McCormick and company, 4449 leads a special *Daylight* train to the New Orleans World's Fair in May 1984. The train is headed east on the SP's Mococco Line just west of Oakley, California.

No. 4449's drivers spin rapidly as she makes 70 miles per hour along Highway 99 headed for Fresno. The Lima superpower locomotive develops her maximum of 5,000 horsepower at 80 miles per hour, giving witness that she truly was designed for high-speed passenger service. The efficiency and lower maintenance costs of diesel-electrics knocked steam engines like 4449 off the rails in the 1950s.

facing back and looking out the conductor's rear window. Everything that you see out that window appears on the engineer's windshield, reflecting off its inside.

During the day, the bright landscape reflects off of it so you get this annoying view that is a composite of half the track ahead and half the view out the conductor's rear window. Very tiring. At night, it's worse. Street lamps and house lights are reflected off the engineer's windshield directly in the track line. Automobiles moving behind you on parallel roads on the conductor's side reflect their headlights and sidemarker lamps off the engineer's windshield. Many times, I have just about gone to emergency because I've seen what appeared to be headlights approaching a crossing and not stopping. EMD really blew the design on those units. It was corrected on later SD60Ms with a two-piece windshield slanted out at the bottom.

Not only have locomotives evolved over the years, many other aspects of railroading in the West have as well. One of the most noteworthy developments was the introduction of marine containers stacked two high in bulkhead or well cars for transporting not only imported goods, but eventually everything from farm produce to auto parts. Many trains now haul nothing but these double-stacks between major West Coast ports and interior cities, and vice-versa. Continuous welded rail replaced jointed steel on all major western mainlines, radio-transmitted track warrants supplanted paper train orders, remote signal control outmoded manned interlocking towers. In short, the entire North American railroad industry, including large and small railroads of the West, has evolved in many ways over the past 30 years, and hopefully will continue its evolution, so that it meets the requirements of the integrated economies it serves.

The Evolution of a Machine

On June 29, 1978, Rock Island EMD F-units equipped for snow-clearing service sit in the carrier's engine facility in Fort Worth, Texas. Engine Nos. 4150 and 4155 are two of Rock Island's 19 F9AMs, which started life as an F3 and F7, respectively, and were later rebuilt by the railroad to 1,750 horsepower. On March 31, 1980, the Rock Island ceased operations and faded into oblivion. *Photo by Lynn Powell*

With her flaking silver paint gleaming in the late afternoon sun, Burlington Northern EMD E8 9949 rips through a small town just south of Auburn, Washington, with a Seattle–Portland Amtrak train in July 1973. The E8 shows the classic "cab" design adopted by the Electro-Motive Division of General Motors for its early passenger diesels. Engine No. 9949 saw many revenue miles pulling the Chicago, Burlington & Quincy's famous *Zephyrs*.

The Evolution of a Machine

Waiting for her next passenger assignment, ex–Delaware & Hudson Alco PA No. 19 idles at Ferrocarril del Pacifico's shops at Empalme, Sonora, in June 1984. She was built as Santa Fe No. 54B in 1947, and was rebuilt by Morrison-Knudsen in 1975. Many rail enthusiasts consider PAs to be the most handsome diesel locomotives ever built.

Sitting in a dead line at Cranbrook, British Columbia, in August 1972, Canadian Pacific "C-liner" 4104 has come to the end of her working days. The CPA16-4 four-axle cab unit built by Fairbanks-Morse affiliate Canadian Locomotive Company in 1954 saw service on CP's Kettle Valley Division. In 1980, CP donated the 4104 to the museum at High River, Alberta.

Santa Fe Alco S2 switcher 2364, built in May 1949, runs around the company's Bakersfield, California, roundhouse on the balloon track in June 1974. For many years, North American railroads consistently purchased diesels designed specifically for switching, but by the 1990s, such purchases had all but ceased. The railroads now use older road locomotives for yard service.

Departing from the ubiquitous cab design of early freight diesels, EMD and its competitors came out with road switchers in the 1950s. SP symbol TRRVY (Tracy, California–Roseville, California, manifest) crosses the wooden trestle at Forest Lake on the afternoon of April 13, 1983. On the point is SD9E 4360, which sports a design virtually identical to EMD's original six-axle road switcher, the SD7. SP took delivery of 43 SD7s starting in 1952, including EMD Demonstrator No. 990.

Northwestern Pacific SD9 4327, ex-SP SD9E 4327, glides past the passenger depot in Petaluma, California, in October 1997. EMD built the road switcher in 1955, one of 150 purchased by the SP. NWP acquired the aging "Cadillac" from OmniTrax in 1996. At one time, SD9s ruled SP's operations in the Tehachapi Mountains; the 4327 proved its worth for the NWP on freights over steep Ridge Hill south of Willits.

The Evolution of a Machine

122 *Chapter 5*

Like EMD, Alco came out with road switcher locomotives, like the four RS3s on a BN transfer run entering the carrier's bridge over the Columbia River at Vancouver, Washington, in August 1972. Built for the Spokane, Portland, & Seattle Railway in the early to mid-1950s, RS3s boasted great visibility and therefore were favorites with switch crews. A handful of these venerable workhorses survived on the BN as late as 1980.

Along with its successful six-axle road switchers, EMD developed a four-axle version, the GP7. Soon thereafter, EMD bumped the horsepower up by 150 and designated the more powerful unit the GP9, like this string of four SP-rebuilt units at Towle on Donner Pass in September 1973. The "Geeps'" 567 non-turbocharged prime movers are screaming in full fury to help lift an eastbound up the 2.1 percent grade.

The Evolution of a Machine   123

Four big Alco DL600B "Alligators" bring a freight out of Northern California into Santa Fe's Barstow Yard in February 1973. Delivered in 1960, No. 9847 saw work in heavy coal service in New Mexico before being assigned to duties on the Valley Line over the Tehachapi Mountains.

A pair of rebuilt Alco 251 prime movers await installation at Ferrocarril del Pacifico's Empalme Shops in Sonora. Designed by the builder as part of its Century line of locomotive products released in 1963, the 251 was also used by Alco's Canadian affiliate, Montreal Locomotive Works, in its M630 and M636 models.

With grass-covered slopes surrounding it, a westbound Santa Fe manifest negotiates the curves at Bealville in Tehachapi Pass in April 1974. The five SD24s on the point represent EMD's answer to Alco's Alligators.

The Evolution of a Machine   125

In 1959, General Electric entered the locomotive market with its landmark U25B diesel-electric. It didn't take GE long to start increasing the horsepower of its products, as evidenced here by two SP U30Cs sandwiched between a pair of U33Cs approaching tunnel No. 2 in Tehachapi Pass at dawn on June 21, 1973. The 3,000-horsepower U30Cs destined for the Bakersfield–Tehachapi freight pool received extra ballast at the factory to increase their pulling power.

Profile in power. A side view of SP U33C 8747 reveals the distinctive "cobra" warning light attached to the cab roof on all of the railroad's GE hood units.

UP GE U30C 2843 leads a Seattle-bound manifest at Vancouver, Washington, in July 1973. Although the EMD SD40-2 far and away ruled the UP during the late 1970s and 1980s, UP bought increasing numbers of GE products after the builder released its more reliable Dash 7 line, which the company premiered at the Chicago Railroad Industry Equipment Show in September 1976. Behind the 2843 is one of UP's GP30Bs—a member of a large fleet of cabless "booster" units the carrier owned—and a pair of 3,600-horsepower SP EMD SD45s, which the builder released in 1965. Until 1972, when GE came out with its U36C, EMD had a corner on the market for high-horsepower, single-engine units.

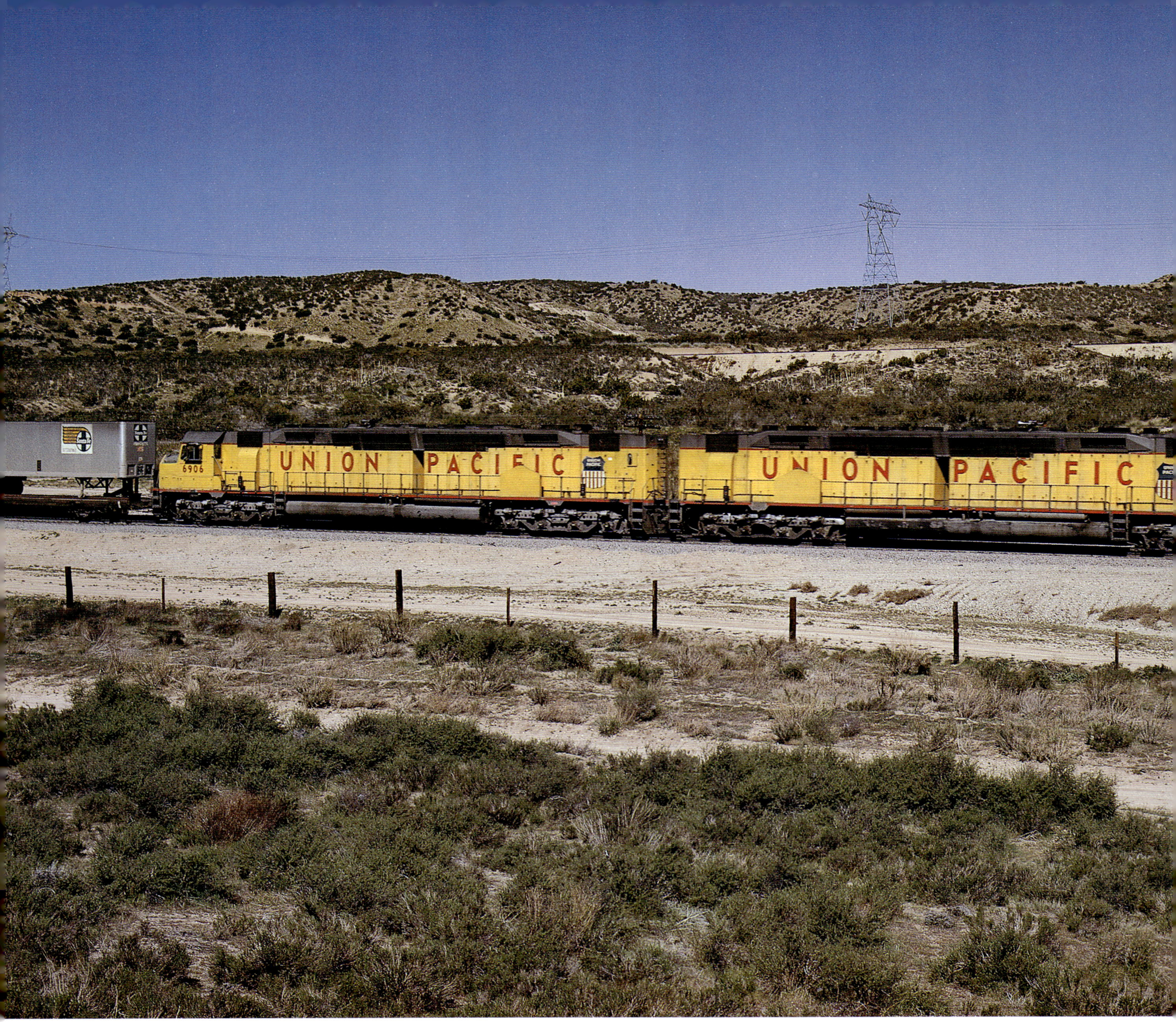
6906
UNION PACIFIC
UNION PACIFIC

A pair of high-hood, steam generator-equipped EMD GP38s has just brought Nacionales de Mexico's *El Tapatio* into Guadalajara Union Station from Mexico City in May 1978. The diesels are typical of EMD's passenger offerings during the 1970s and 1980s, when freight diesels ruled the roost and passenger orders were few and far between.

Dropping off the eastern slope of Cajon Pass in April 1974, UP's hot *LAX* piggyback train is doing all of track speed behind a pair of back-to-back, double-diesel EMD DDA40X Centennials. By 1968 EMD was already planning what was sure to be the 50 series, with the standard 16-cylinder 645 boosted up from 3,000 horsepower to 3,300 horsepower. Although there were some pretty strong indications from the field that the customers weren't really interested in more horsepower, UP's chief mechanical officer, Dave Neuhart, asked for another big engine. His timing was perfect: EMD had some ideas along that line and was looking for a way to try them out. In cooperation with Neuhart and his staff, EMD designed and produced the first DDA40X within 13 months, just in time for the centennial celebration of the completion of the first transcontinental railroad. It was a radical machine in many ways, conceived and executed to be as maintenance-free as possible while supplying maximum output.

The Evolution of a Machine

At one time hundreds of railroad interlocking towers dotted North America where the rail lines of two or more carriers intersected. With the advent of ground-relay radio communication and sophisticated telemetry, the need for towers was obviated. Stockton Tower, which for many decades protected the Santa Fe's Valley Line and mainlines of the SP and WP/UP, is now just a patch of ground replaced by Centralized Traffic Control (CTC) signals.

130 Chapter 5

Before the advent of widespread radio communication in the railroad industry, paper train orders, or "flimsies," hooped up to train crews by operators were the most common way of transferring track authority in non-CTC territory. In June 1974, the engineer and conductor of Santa Fe 3345 West both pick up orders at Stockton Tower which will tell them of any meets they'll have across the San Joaquin Delta.

The Evolution of a Machine   131

A string of UP EMD GP9As and Bs departs the carrier's yard in Spokane, Washington, in August 1973 and comes out onto the Spokane International mainline. As soon as the lead Geep steps onto the mainline, the indicator attached to the near signal mast will go "horizontal."

RIGHT: Leaving Amboy, California, behind, a westbound Santa Fe piggyback train continues its crossing of the Mojave Desert in October 1982. Within three years the caboose on its rear will have disappeared from all trains, replaced by a small electronic box known as an end-of-train device.

In 1974, SP started to experiment with the Locotrol remote-control system, in which helper locomotives could be controlled via radio signals. The railroad received 14 SD40T-2s specially fitted with 116-inch noses to accommodate the Locotrol radio equipment, seven being "masters" and the remaining seven "slaves." In March 1975, 8302 East storms through Bealville, California, with a master "snoot" on the point and an unmanned slave leading the swing helper. SP's distinctive trackside indicators are still in evidence.

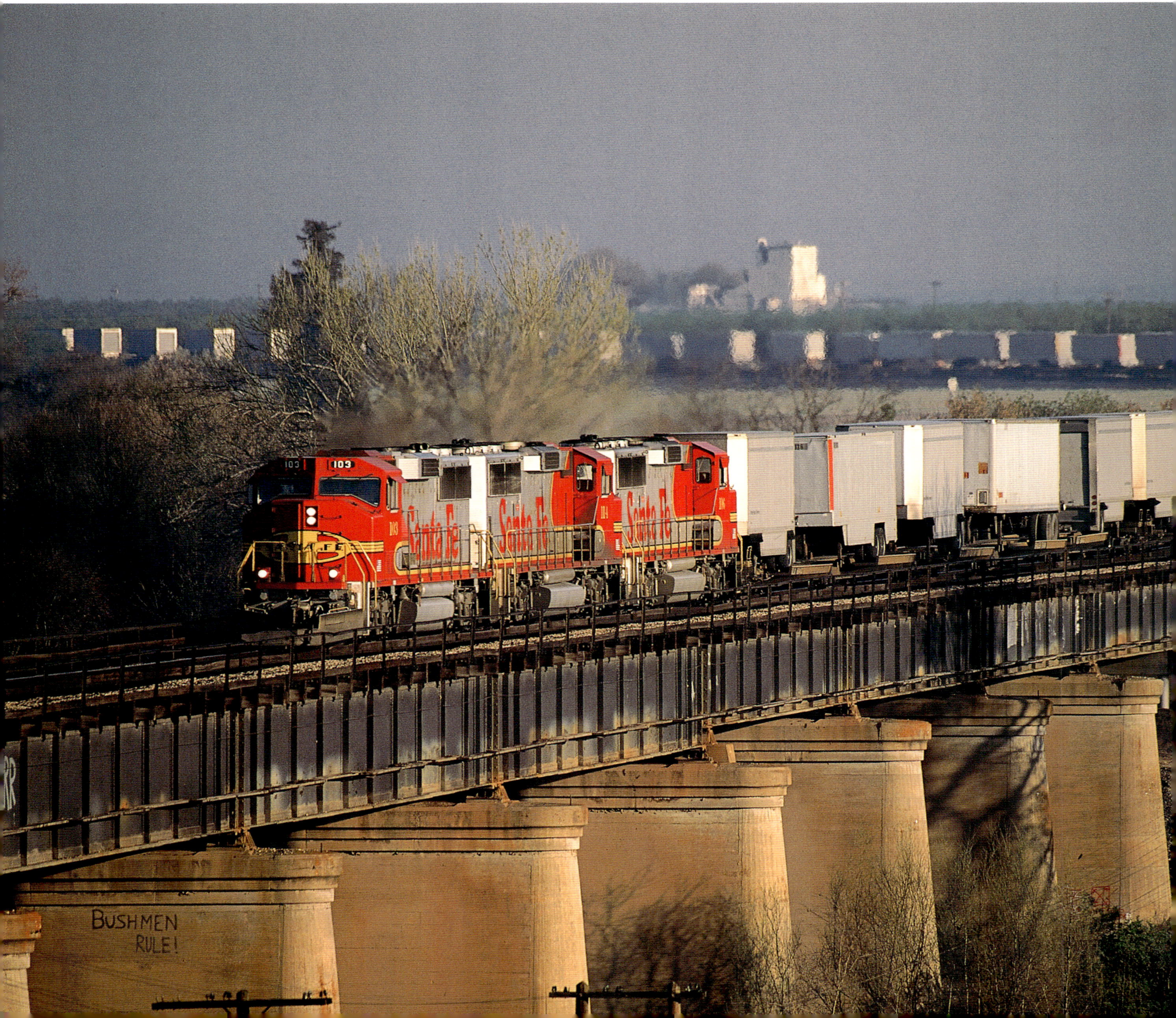

Santa Fe
Santa Fe
Santa Fe
103
BUSHMEN
RULE!

Three red-and-silver Santa Fe EMD GP60Ms have a long string of United Parcel Service trailers rolling across the Merced River Bridge at Ballico, California, on a beautiful spring morning in March 1991. A good portion of the 991 train consists of articulated spine cars, which feature lower tare weight than conventional equipment and very little slack action; this means the carrier will save fuel and will damage less customer goods en route to Chicago.

As early as 1984, American President Lines (APL) experimented with UP on the concept of stacking two containers in a railcar, while Sea-Land began running double-stack container trains on SP's Coast Route. It proved to be a revolution in intermodal railroading, decreasing customers' shipping costs and lowering railroad revenues in the short run. In August 1996, ex-C&NW GE Dash 9 8623 leads a hot APL double-stack train at Wyche, California. In another 30 minutes, the stack train will be climbing the Coast Range through Altamont Pass, headed for the Port of Oakland.

The Evolution of a Machine 135

136 Chapter 5

By the time Amtrak went shopping for new locomotives to replace its aging fleet of EMD F40s, North American passenger unit design had changed radically. GE P42 GENESIS locomotive 159 on the point of the eastbound *Sunset Limited* at Tucson, Arizona, wearing the carrier's Phase V paint scheme, typifies the look of new passenger diesels in the West since the 1990s. The GENESIS units sport a European appearance, with a monocoque body designed in conjunction with Krupp of Germany.

The wide-cab design pioneered on EMD's DDA40X over 30 years ago, complete with two-piece windshield, survives on even the most modern UP locomotive, the SD70M. Here, newly delivered UP No. 4983 heads into a spectacular sunset at the east end of Tucson Yard in August 2002. Despite the door in the nose and the desktop control panel inside, the design is essentially the same as on the DDs. Also, the canted radiators on the rear of the SD70M are reminiscent of those on the Centennials.

The Evolution of a Machine   137

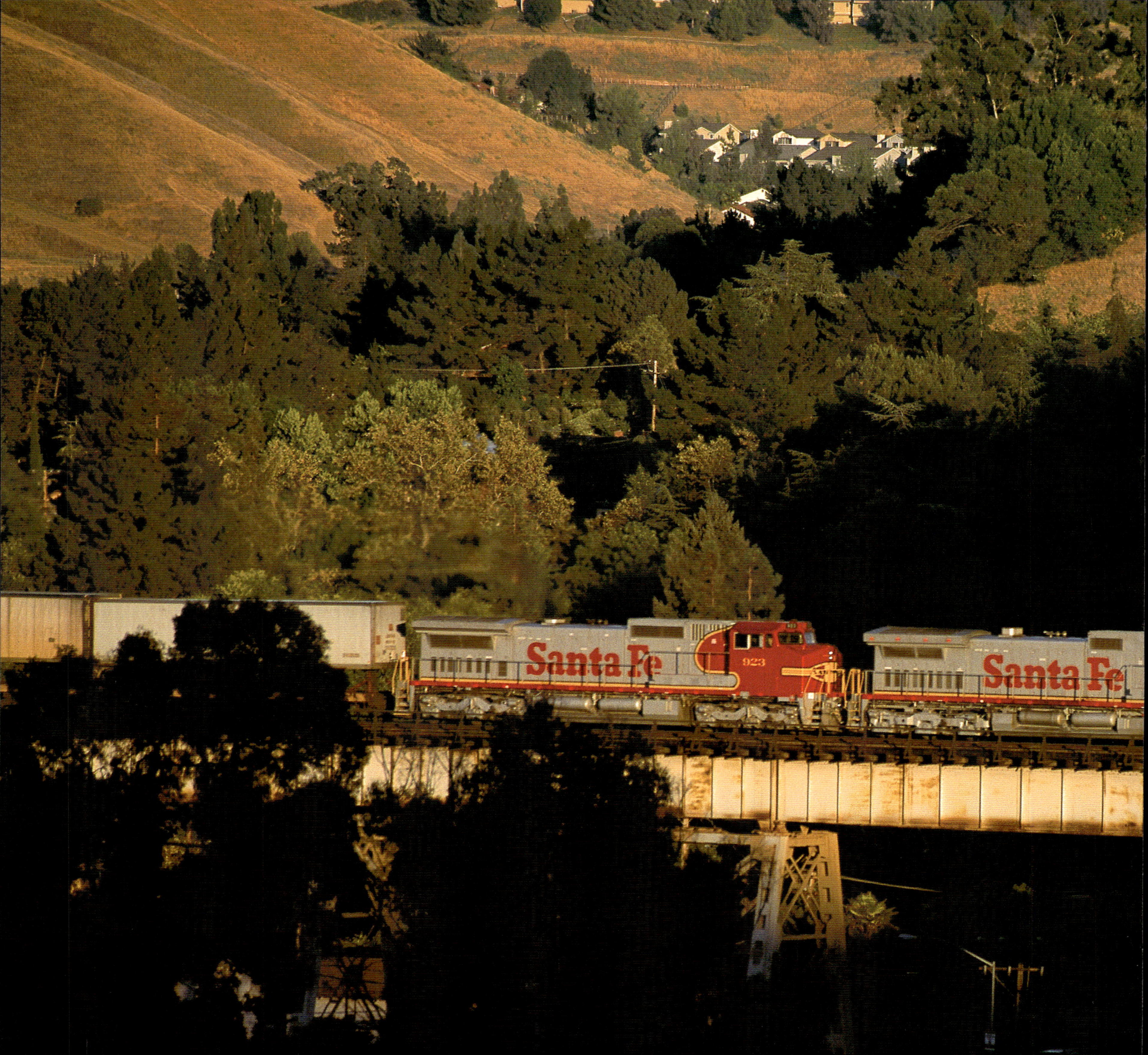
Santa Fe
923
Santa Fe

Chapter Six

MEMORIES *from the* MOUNTAINS

"Mojave Sub dispatcher to ATSF 2913 East. I'm gonna have to put you in at Sanborn for two wests. The 9-199 is out of Jim Gray."

Not long after 2913 heads into the siding out of view beyond a ridge to the west, a long, shimmering mirage appears beyond hundreds of acres of sagebrush. The 199 roars by uphill, followed shortly by another train, a fast-moving 899.

"2913, I'm gonna take you over to Bissell to meet two more wests, and then I'll let you go." The stack train no sooner gets up a head of steam than its engineer backs off on the throttle and rolls into the Centralized Traffic Controlled siding that's brought him only 6-1/2 miles further east from Sanborn. A little under an hour later, after a San Joaquin Valley–bound grain train blasts by, the dispatcher advises 2913 that he'll be there for a 985, a hot eastbound that'll run around him, and then he can get on the move. Seems the second westbound, whatever it is, has been delayed.

The 2913, an eastbound stack in the hole, has plenty of power this morning, including the aging GP35 out front, a pair of Burlington Northern SD40-2s, a Santa Fe SD45-2B, and a sparkling Conrail SD60. Whatever he's got in those J.B. Hunt containers must not be time-sensitive—the dispatcher is giving precedence to trains that are probably slightly hotter or whose crews will perhaps go "dead on the law" sooner. BNSF's been running the wheels off its locomotives lately, and the number of engineers in the Barstow pool has skyrocketed. But the railroad's physical plant will handle only so many trains, and the Mojave Sub is single-track—when there's lots of traffic and you're not on a "shooter," you sit or leapfrog from siding to siding. Finally, the 985 streaks around the huge curve that bends from northwest to northeast, and leaves nothing but blowing sand behind. In a few minutes, 2913 leaves on a green.

Before the stack train's rear cars clear the switch, another east man creeps up toward the signals guarding 2913's departure. The dispatcher must be chomping at the bit! He's probably been holding the 985 and this second hot train, fresh off Tehachapi's 2.2 percent grade, at Mojave for the 899 and the grain movement. Once he's turned 'em loose, he's not leaving any more space between them than absolutely necessary. After the eastbound trio disappears over the horizon toward Boron, the mysterious west man finally shows—and puts on a show! It's a heavy KCPB (Kansas City to Pittsburg, California) coiled-steel drag with six SD40-2s, four up front and two that he picked up at Edwards pushing on the rear, with a BN white-face leading, and an equal number of ATSF and BN units throughout. The coiled steel is bound for the U.S. Steel-POSCO plant just west of the San Joaquin Delta, but before it can get there it'll have to cross these mountains in the Mojave Desert and then the Tehachapis.

Mountains. They riddle the entire face of western North America, a fact of life railroads have had to deal with since they came to the region. In the days of steam, helper districts dotted the West, and some, like those on Donner, Soldier Summit, Tehachapi, the Needles Subdivision, Marias Pass, and the Lordsburg District, still persist. Even with cutting-edge technology, engineers need to be especially vigilant in mountain territory. According to Doug Harrop, veteran mountain engineer:

> The GEs, old and new, have "throttle lag," and it is even greater on the newer units. An example: come off the Montello Hill with two UP 7500s (C60ACs) and go out of dynamic brake at the foot of the grade at 40, 50, or 60 miles per hour. Come out in power, and it is a full two minutes or more before any power can be felt. By then you have lost 10 or more miles per hour—very frustrating, especially when you do not dare exceed the speed limit, a very fireable offense. Power is almost immediate on EMD models, even at higher speeds.
>
> The new computerized AC units are OK now, but had many software glitches when first introduced. It was wild when the computer went down for no apparent reason on the middle of the hill, and Mr. Goodwrench in Omaha would run through a list of things to boot it up, none of which usually worked. This still happens, but not as often. Of course, there was, and is, a comfort level with the old units. When they went down, you fixed them, usually on the move. This is not generally possible with the new power. It is like looking under the hood of a new car. I did this with my new auto two weeks ago and wondered where the battery was. Turns out you have to remove the right front wheel to access the battery! [As with many new automobiles], you do not repair the new locomotives with cut-in-half fusees, broken flag sticks, and duct tape.

Gene Lawson, retired Milwaukee Road engineer, relates the following regarding his experiences on the Coast Division running locomotives that were decades older than the ones referred to by Harrop:

> My dad, Lloyd L. Lawson, started his career on the Milwaukee Road in 1918 with a crew installing equipment in the Kittitas, Washington, Substation. My mother was the cook in the crews' dining car that was coupled together with the bunk cars near the substation. [When the railroad] began operation of the electrification in

PREVIOUS PAGES: Brand-new Santa Fe GE Dash 9 No. 644 and Dash 8 companion 923 roar across Muir Trestle in Martinez, California, as the shadows of the Coast Range begin to engulf the Alhambra Valley. It's June 1994, and the Santa Fe's red-and-silver warbonnet paint scheme is alive and well. No. 644 West is in the midst of a 1.0 percent climb to the crest of the Coast Range in Franklin Canyon. The summit lies inside Tunnel No. 3, the longest on the entire Santa Fe.

1920, my dad bid on a substation job at Taunton, Washington, which is about 10 miles west of Othello. In 1932, we moved to Kittitas, where he was substation operator until 1960, when he retired with 42 years on the Milwaukee Road.

I hired out as a fireman August 15, 1950, with seniority between Cle Elum, Washington, and Avery, Idaho. My duties were to help the engineer by checking [the boxcab electric] trailing units to make sure everything was working properly and that bearings weren't running hot. If they needed packing, that was my job. After a couple years, the engineers I teamed with put me to work running the locomotives, switching the trains at Othello, and running the trains over the road.

According to Lawson, aside from handling the *Olympian Hiawatha*, which the railroad discontinued in 1961, his favorite job was running the electrics. "They were great for handling trains over mountain territory," he recalls. Toward the end of their lives in the 1970s, the electrics, according to Lawson, started "falling down," and the company had to make replacement parts for them in their own shops, or cannibalize sidelined electrics to keep the others going. Gene recalls that two sets of four-unit boxcabs descending Boylston Hill in Washington created enough power with their regenerative braking to light the entire Kittitas Valley.

Lawson was promoted to engineer in 1957, and his first assignment was in electric motor E-47, on a freight out of Ellensburg. He laid down a generous portion of sand, gave the electric all the juice she could handle, and tore out of town with his charge. In so doing, he drew a tremendous amount of power from the Kittitas Substation, enough to bring the operator's ire down on top of him for the jackrabbit start. On several occasions, Lawson worked the electric helper set stationed at Beverly, where the 17-mile, 2.2 percent climb up the Saddle Mountains to Boylston, the steepest grade on the railroad, began. The peak time for the electric utility that served the Milwaukee in the area was from 5 to 6 P.M., and to avoid the high rates during that hour, railroad management had all electric-powered trains head into sidings.

Lawson recalls an interesting mishap his first year as an engineer. A freight had just started down the hill from Boylston, and before the crew was able to set the brakes, a casting or pin broke between the front and rear units of the electric locomotive. The front units took off down the hill and left the tracks on the first curve below Dorris. The head brakeman had been riding in the rear unit, and upon realizing something was wrong, made a dash for the lead cab, only to find the wide-open spaces when he opened the unit's blind-end door."

Bill Plattenberger, division superintendent of the Milwaukee Road's Rocky Mountain Division from 1965 to 1970, offers a glimpse into the operation of the railroad's two hottest freight trains through his territory in the 1960s and 1970s: Nos. 261 and 262, otherwise known as the *Thunderhawk* and the *XL Special*, respectively:

> Schedules, blocking, locomotive consist, load restrictions, length and tonnage of trains, pick up and set out points, et cetera, on transcontinental trains such as 261 and 262 were developed and monitored by the general manager's office in Chicago, and from time to time changes were made to meet marketing department objectives. Division personnel were not authorized to make changes in the advertised schedules, train handling, and so forth. Trains 261 and 262 were the top priority trains on the railroad, and in single-track territory, such as the Rocky Mountain Division, held the main track at meeting or passing stations, and other trains were to be clear of the main track sufficiently in advance of 261 and 262 to avoid delay.
>
> At crew change points, crews were called ahead of the arrival time to allow them to read the bulletin board, check train orders, check and fill out the train register, and be standing on the platform when the train arrived. At 500-mile inspection points, such as Miles City and Deer Lodge, Montana, the mechanical department had car and locomotive personnel positioned to commence their inspection and servicing immediately on arrival. If the train was to arrive at the time mechanical department personnel would normally be changing crews, the shift would be held on duty and incur overtime, rather than delay the train because of a shift change. To minimize the chances of setting out bad order cars, 261 and

262 did not carry open-top loads or friction-bearing equipment, and locomotive power was assigned to operate through between Chicago and Tacoma, with a [Little] Joe being added to the head end of the consist between Harlowton, Montana, and Avery, Idaho, to help maintain the schedule through the mountain territory.

How do the newer EMDs and GEs fair in heavy freight service in mountainous territory? Harrop shares some experiences from the mountains of northeastern Nevada. "Our 'testing grounds' for power are the 20-mile Montello Hill, ruling grade of 1.5 percent, and the 10-mile Wells Hill, 1.4 percent, both twisting through many curves," he explains. "Both hills have 8,700-ton coupler limits [for conventional equipment], and 11,000 tons for high-strength equipment [grain, coal trains, etc.]. Two [SD9043MAC] 4,300-horsepower units are frequently assigned to 8,700-ton trains, 1 horsepower per ton. They walk the trains up Montello Hill at 7 to 9 miles per hour. Two 6,000-horsepower GEs [1.4 horsepower per ton] do no better on such trains and are notorious slippers. The additional horsepower does not, apparently, mean more tractive effort." This is a significant point, considering that the difference in horsepower would be 3,400, more than that of an SD40-2! "Perhaps this is why the UP is ordering SD70 DC power for general service," Harrop offers.

Harrop goes on to offer this tactile comparison of old versus newer EMDs and GEs:

I will give the new units this: They are very much quieter, warm in winter, cool in summer, and in general, ride better. But they cannot, with their quiet efficiency, begin to match the thrill that comes with accelerating out of town on a quartet of SD45s. The sound, even the feel, was just terrific, and we enjoyed it so much that most of us with 20 or more years in are 60 percent deaf. And speaking of sounds, try this sometime: Find a place where crews change and the outbound crew can kick off the air and accelerate out of town. On a cold winter night, a set of four-cycle GEs makes the best sound, in my opinion, in all of railroading. It was even better with the "crack-crack-crack" of U30Cs. Try it sometime and see if you don't agree. Westbound out of Elko, Nevada, is a good place to do this.

I am gradually—but not completely, never completely—being won over to the new units. They are better in some, but certainly not all, ways. It is true that the new power will never give me the thrill of coming to work and still finding, once in a while, an SD45 or U33C on the point of my train. Why not? We go back 30-plus years together.

With acrid smoke from brake shoes spilling into the forest, a westbound BN freight emerges from Cascade Tunnel at the top of Stevens Pass in August 1972. In 1925, Great Northern began construction on the present 7.79-mile tunnel to replace the original 2.63-mile bore completed in 1900. At a cost of $26 million, the new bore was completed in approximately four years, and on January 12, 1929, GN's westbound *Oriental Limited* was the first train to pass through it.

142   Chapter 6

A big GE U33C leads a Burlington Northern mixed freight eastward through Washington's Stevens Pass in July 1973. This line was part of James J. Hill's Great Northern Railway, which was completed between St. Paul, Minnesota, and Seattle on January 6, 1893. After Hill decided in 1890 to extend the Great Northern to the Pacific, he hired John F. Stevens to do the job.

A trio of EMD SD45s wait to meet a westbound freight before heading east into Cascade Tunnel with their manifest in August 1972. Originally an electrified bore, Stevens Pass saw its last electric-powered train on July 31, 1956.

Memories from the Mountain

An assortment of early and late second-generation power is on the point of this westbound Santa Fe freight as it approaches Tunnel No. 2 in Tehachapi Pass in August 1973. Santa Fe always assigned its most powerful locomotives to the Tehachapis, including, in their turn, EMD SD24s and Alco DL600Bs (a.k.a. "Alligators"), followed later by EMD SD45s, F45s, SD45-2s, and GE U36Cs.

After tacking two sets of light helpers onto the point of a Santa Fe westbound in the north siding at Woodford, the crew is about to mount the cab of the lead SD45 and depart on signal indication for Bakersfield. The Santa Fe power and train have met two trains here in the last 15 minutes, the first a giant Southern Pacific manifest with a slave swing helper, and the second a Santa Fe led by an F45.

Peering through a 500-millimeter lens from Woodford, the first siding west of the Tehachapi Loop, affords a great view as an eastbound Santa Fe intermodal train plies both the Loop and its approach simultaneously. A shiny GP60M in the consist catches the last rays of the setting sun as it rounds this engineering marvel, hatched in the mind of SP's famed civil engineer, William Hood.

On a frosty morning in January 1983, Western Pacific EMD GP40-2 No. 3519 leads train symbol *WPE* through Chilcoot, California. Although UP officially took control of WP the previous month, WP power is still found in force on ex-WP rails. Unlike rival SP, WP opted to purchase four-axle road power exclusively, both from EMD and GE.

146

LEFT: With a mix of motive power and paint schemes, WP 3015 East sends the vibrations of its diesels' prime movers echoing through the lower Feather River Canyon in June 1974. The water level of the river is high this year, indicating a good snow pack at higher elevations. Water cascading down the canyon walls may also lead to rockslides, a constant danger the railroad has to deal with.

In June 1974, WP 3529 East climbs through Spring Garden, California, toward the longest tunnel on the railroad. The water flowing along the left side of the right-of-way emanates from a spring inside the tunnel, giving the location its name.

Memories from the Mountain 147

At Verdi, Nevada, SP's Nos. 1 and 2 tracks are reversed, with No. 2 on the north. Late in the afternoon in January 1975, an ex-SP FP7 leads the *San Francisco Zephyr* through Verdi, only a few minutes from a crew change in Sparks. Once at Sparks, the FP7 helper will be cut off, and the SDP40Fs will take the *Zephyr* across the Great Basin Desert to Ogden, Utah, on its way to Chicago.

High in the Sierra Nevada, the sky is a deep blue and the air refreshingly brisk as Amtrak EMD SDP40F 585 and a mate roll the eastbound *San Francisco Zephyr* through Cisco in October 1974. The big cowls sport dual horns mounted directly over each windshield, providing more than enough sound to get passengers' attention at station platforms and motorists' attention at grade crossings. In 1985, Santa Fe acquired 18 of the big cowl units for freight service, later adding a notch to either side of the short hood, and handrails to the front to make it easier to change crews "on the fly."

A swing helper consisting of an EMD SD40, two SD45s, and an SD45T-2 assists an SP eastbound fruit block up the Donner grade at Towle in September 1973. SP purchased scores of Tunnel Motors to overcome overheating problems in the Sierra tunnels and snowsheds. The Tunnel Motor design allowed faster cooling once the locomotive was outside of a bore or shed, thus helping to avoid the cumulative heating and concomitant engine shutdown problems endemic to the standard SD45 configuration.

Four EMD 20-cylinder, 3,600-horsepower locomotives blast up the 2.4 percent grade on No. 1 track at Newcastle, California, in September 1973. On February 18, 1864, Leland Stanford and Mark Hopkins took 30 dignitaries in an open-air passenger car to the end of the 16 miles of track then laid, and then on to Newcastle and Bloomer Cut by carriage. Among the riders was *Sacramento Union* editor Lauren Upson, who reported that the Central Pacific's cuts and fills in the 7 miles just west of Newcastle were as great as any in the nation, and that there would be no steeper grade anywhere in the Sierra crossing.

Memories from the Mountain 151

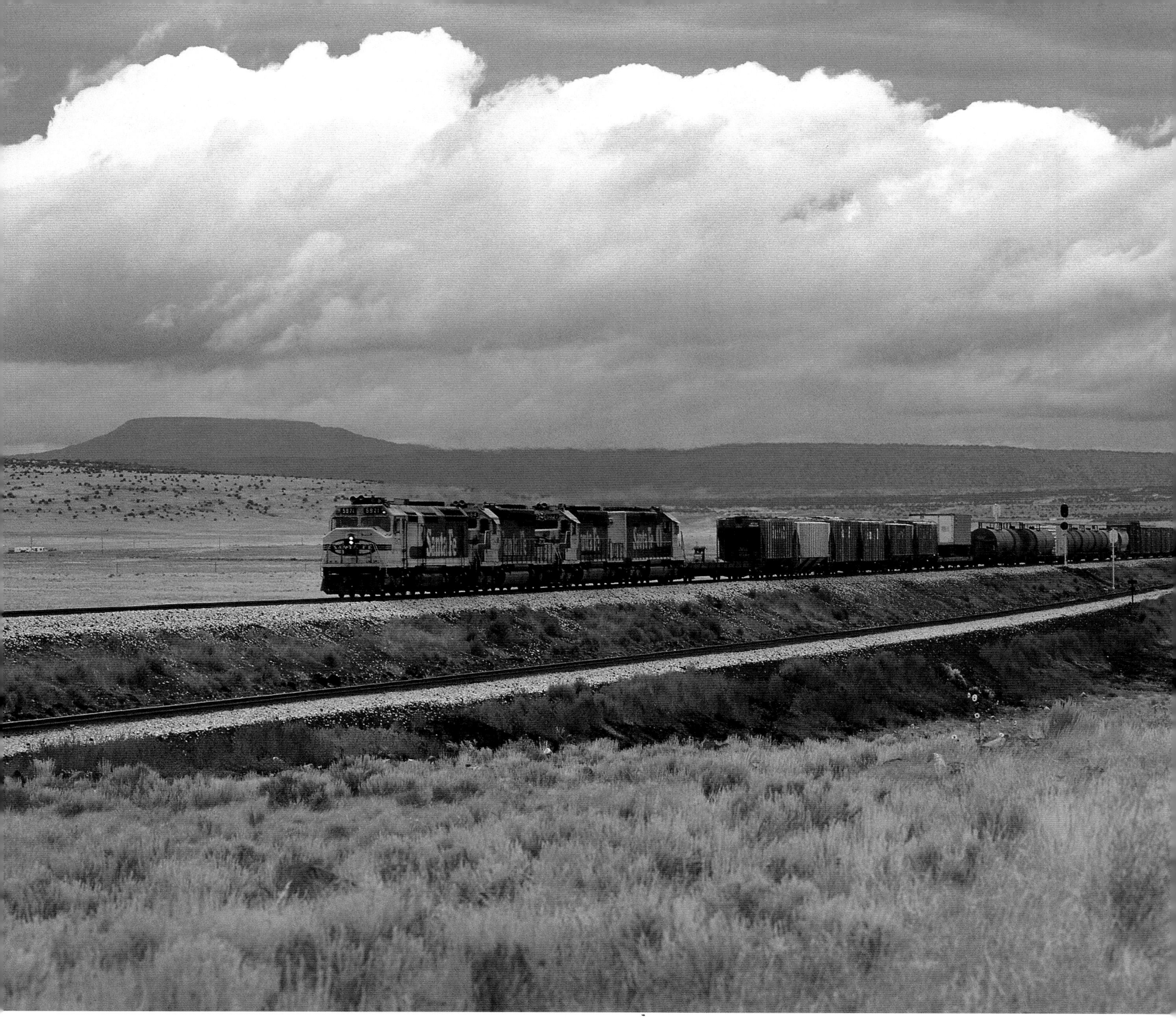
Santa Fe
Santa Fe
Santa Fe

Shrouded by a monsoon cloud layer left over from the previous day's thunderstorms, the little town of Darling on the eastern flank of the Arizona Divide is awakened by the sound of a K5 horn on the morning of July 16, 1985. Amtrak train No. 4, the *Southwest Chief*, is burning up the ballast as it leaves Flagstaff and the San Francisco Mountains behind.

With monsoon skies gathering fury overhead on July 18, 1985, a Santa Fe 804 train headed for Denver climbs the south track out of Seligman, Arizona. Only a few months previously, the railroad had eliminated Seligman as a crew change point, which had a devastating impact on the small town's already frail economy. But to this day, it is still a favorite stop for aficionados of Route 66, and it limps along with a couple of colorful restaurants and a handful of vintage motels.

Memories from the Mountain 153

With a pair of EMD SD9s and a GP9 for power, a Northwestern Pacific passenger excursion makes its way north along California Highway 101 amidst the hills and the mountains of the Coast Range. It's October 1996, and a couple of years hence the fledgling carrier resurrected on the rails of the Southern Pacific property of the same name will find itself in dire straits after massive rains undermine the right-of-way in a number of locations. As a result, the Federal Railroad Administration officially shut the railroad down in 1998.

Returning from Willits, an NWP passenger special passes southbound through the verdant grape vineyards of California's wine country at Asti near sundown. The train is headed back to its jump-off point of Healdsburg in this portrait captured in October 1996. SP completed construction of the original NWP in 1914, and in 1984 sold part of it to businessman Bryan Wipple, who ran the northern end of the railroad as the Eureka Southern. After Wipple filed for bankruptcy two years later, the North Coast Railroad Authority purchased the entire property in 1992 and formed the new NWP.

Catching the last rays of the sun, the NWP insignia on the railroad's offices at Schelleville, California, the railroad's southern terminus, shows its depiction of a redwood tree, the Pacific Ocean, and the Coast Range, all very apparent elements along its 314-mile line.

A westbound Denver & Rio Grande Western manifest with its dynamic braking engaged drops down the 2.0 percent grade at the Gilluly "loops" in June 1989. One hundred years earlier to the month, the Rio Grande Western Railway was organized to convert the narrow-gauge D&RGW, which ran from Ogden, Utah, to Grand Junction, Colorado, to standard gauge.

Rio Grande 5333 West has just changed crews at Helper, Utah, and now attacks the 8.5-mile, 2.4 percent grade to Kyune. A mine near the dramatic rock formation owned and operated by Utah Fuel produces high-quality coal. On March 8, 1923, a huge explosion in No. 2 mine at Castle Gate took the lives of 173 men. Since then, safety and working conditions have improved substantially.

Leaning into a curve on the South Track between Lugo and Hesperia, an eastbound Santa Fe manifest that's also dead-heading power back to Barstow, rolls off Cajon Pass' eastern slope at track speed in November 1974. Unlike many other Class I railroads that shied away from EMD's 20-cylinder engine when a problem surfaced from the manner in which the A-frames supporting the crankshaft were welded to the crankcase, Santa Fe ordered a goodly number of SD45-2s, as evidenced by seven such units in this consist. Max Ephraim, design engineer for EMD at the time, states that although the problem was fixed as soon as he found out about it, the perception remained in the minds of Class I mechanical forces: the 20-cylinder prime mover was prone to crankcase weld problems. In his words, "Railroads have memories like elephants—real long ones."

In August 1982, a string of six EMD SD40-2s and a GE U30C roar through a reverse curve on the east side of California's Cajon Pass as they speed a long consist of piggyback trailers toward Los Angeles. Union Pacific 3279 West is following a route once known as the Old Spanish Trail. After having been discharged from the U.S. Army, members of the Mormon Battalion led by Jefferson Hunt traveled to the Salt Lake Valley in 1848, forming the first cattle drive through Cajon Pass.

RIGHT: Little Joe E-70, with no trace of exhaust, leads two EMD SD40-2s and an SD45 pouring diesel smoke into the clean air at Avery, Idaho, with an eastbound fruit block loaded with perishables harvested from Washington's fertile lands. By June 15, 1974, all electric operations on the Milwaukee Road ceased, closing one of the most interesting chapters in all of western North American railroading.

With a Little Joe on the point as helper for its trip up St. Paul Pass and the Bitterroot Mountains, an eastbound Milwaukee Road freight crosses over the St. Joe River at Steel Bridge in August 1973. Behind the Joe are EMD SD40-2s—some with winterized windows, some without—that will take the freight to Chicago. Milwaukee's St. Paul Pass line contained 11 massive steel trestles like this one at Steel Bridge, an indication of the challenge and cost the railroad faced in building its line through this rugged country.

158   Chapter 6

In August 1973, a Milwaukee Road eastbound glides over the St. Regis River at St. Regis, Montana. After leaving the confines of St. Paul Pass via the horseshoe curve at Bryson, the Milwaukee's mainline joined the course of the St. Regis River and followed it for a good 20 miles. This watercourse afforded the railroad a relatively easy construction path, compared to the Herculean challenges it faced immediately to the west.

Memories from the Mountain 159

In August 1973, Milwaukee Road GE EF-1 locomotive E-45 helps an eastbound merchandise freight over Pipestone Pass east of Butte, Montana. There are crews in both the boxcab and the lead diesel, since the E-45 will cut off on the other side of the summit and return light to Butte. Built by General Electric between September 1915 and January 1917, Milwaukee's EF-1 freight locomotives were only capable of 30 miles per hour, but proved to be some of the most rugged and reliable machines ever to ride the rails.

Once cut off from the eastbound it helped over Pipestone Pass, E-45 prepares to enter the siding and let the manifest pass. Her brakeman will shortly climb off the ancient electric to throw the switch.

Arriving back in Butte, E-45's brakeman climbs down off the aging locomotive to line the switch back to the engine facility. It is strange to think that no track, signal, nor catenary remains as a memorial to the men and women who worked the Milwaukee's Pacific Extension.

After meeting a westbound at sunset, the engineer at the helm of SP's loaded "oil cans" states clearly over the radio to his helper engineer, "We have a green." He then notches out the throttle and brings his train through the east switch of Bealville siding onto the mainline, the helpers at the far right of the image doing their part to move the 10,000-ton train up the steep grade. It's November 1993, and the unit oil train will soon be replaced by a pipeline running over the Tehachapis.

SP symbol BRLAT (Brooklyn Yard, Oregon–Los Angeles, Trailers) roars uphill on the double track at Cable a few miles below the summit of Tehachapi Pass on July 19, 1978. To help the piggyback train keeps its hot schedule, another "snoot" SD40T-2 was tacked on the rear of the train behind the caboose at Bakersfield to raise its horsepower-per-ton ratio.

Memories from the Mountain 163

Santa Fe symbol 199, the railroad's hottest train, running on a super-tight, 52-hour Chicago–Richmond, California, schedule, charges up the grade in Franklin Canyon toward Tunnel No. 3 on the afternoon of April 20, 1989. Engine No. 7400 was an experimental testbed design built by GE in 1984 that proved a precursor to the subsequent Dash 8 line of locomotives that allowed the builder to capture most of the market from rival EMD.

On July 19, 1985, under monsoon skies, Santa Fe's three GE B39-8 testbeds, 7400–7402, roll a westbound intermodal train toward the eastern entrance to Arizona's Crozier Canyon. Santa Fe retired the three B39s in November 1992, returning them to GE. Unit 7400 later saw service on Conrail. Crozier Canyon is home to some important Americana, including the Beale Wagon Road and Route 66.

The sun has set at Palmer Lake, Colorado, as two BNSF loaded coal trains headed for Texas converge on the tiny mountain town. UP's WR-86 dispatcher has southbound trains running on both No. 1 and No. 2 track this evening on the Joint Line; No.1 is usually used for northbound movements. After the train at left on No. 1 tops the grade and begins its descent to Colorado Springs, the dispatcher will give the train on No. 2 track a green light to follow it.

With an ex-Conrail B36-7 in its consist, UP 9738 East pulls hard through a long, sweeping curve up the 1.0 percent grade at Shawmut, Arizona, on the Sunset Route. On this crisp April morning in 2000, the Sand Tank Mountains loom in the distance as the train's mix of containers and autoracks slices through groves of palo verdes, saguaros, and mesquites. It will be another 10 minutes before the eastbound reaches the summit at Estrella in its 19-mile climb out of Gila Bend.

Index

Alco (American Locomotive Company), 13, 21, 35, 36, 39, 46, 63, 68, 80, 83, 92, 118, 119, 123, 124, 144
    DL600B "Alligators", 124, 125, 144
    PA, 118
    RS3, 123
    S2 switcher, 119
Amador Foothills Railroad, 54
American President Lines (APL), 135
Amtrak, 7, 14, 22, 23, 30, 32, 75, 84, 85, 94, 149, 153
    Denver Zephyr, 30
    EMD SDP40F, 32
    Southwest Chief, 7, 32, 153
    San Francisco Zephyr, 22, 23, 30, 32, 148, 149
    San Joaquin, 14, 75, 85
ASARCO's Ray Mine, 31, 32, 76. See also Santa Fe Railway
Atchison, Topeka & Santa Fe (AT&SF), 12, 30, 60. *See also* Santa Fe Railway
    ATSF 2913, 139, 140

Benson, Ted, 91
Brotherhood of Locomotive Firemen and Enginemen's Magazine, The, 112
Browning, Sue, 104, 105
Burlington Northern (BN), 7, 9, 13, 16, 30, 48, 50, 60, 63, 64, 82, 83, 91, 114, 123, 140, 142, 143
Burlington Northern Santa Fe (BNSF), 33, 48, 75, 78, 79, 114, 140, 166, 167

Cab design, 114, 117, 120, 137
California Department of Transportation (Caltrans), 14
Canadian Locomotive Company, 119
Canadian National (CN), 12, 103
    Supercontinental, 103
Canadian Pacific, 11, 12, 24, 25, 46, 119
    The Canadian, 25
Central Pacific, 10, 150
Centralized Traffic Control (CTC), 55, 64, 90, 130, 131, 139
Chicago, Burlington & Quincy *Zephyr*, 117
Chicago, Milwaukee, St. Paul & Pacific, 12
Chicago, Rock Island & Pacific, 12
Coifman, Ben, 111, 112
Container-on-flatcar (COFC), 85
Copper Basin Railway (CBRY), 31, 32, 76, 77
Crocker, Charly, 10

Denver & Rio Grande Western, 12, 20, 30, 52, 73, 156
    EMD SD40T-2, 20
    EMD SD50, 20
    Railblazer, 52
Dewald, Darrel, 66, 90
Dezendorf, N. C., 112

EMC (Electro-Motive Corporation), 111, 112, 113, 117
    FT (freight twenty-seven hundred horsepower), 112

EMD, 18, 32, 39, 43–45, 50, 53, 60, 68, 72, 91, 104, 112–116, 120, 123, 125, 129, 132, 133, 135, 140, 142, 146, 150, 157, 158, 164
    Dash 2 series, 18, 91, 113
    DDA40X, 18, 83, 91, 129, 136, 137
    E8, 117
    F7A, 109
    F7B, 30
    F40, 137
    FP45, 50
    FT diesel-electrics, 55
    GP7, 123
    GP9, 18, 100, 122, 123, 132, 154
    GP38, 129
    GP40, 50, 91
    SD7, 120
    SD9, 121, 154
    SD24, 125, 144
    SD40, 30, 150
    SD40-2, 50, 51, 60, 67, 91, 140, 142, 144, 146, 157, 158
    SD40T-2, 30, 33, 83, 56, 8–10, 73, 91, 133, 150, 163
    SD45, 30, 45, 51, 113, 114, 144, 145, 150, 158
    SD60, 91, 140
    SD60M, 114, 115, 134, 135
    SD70M, 18, 86, 97, 104, 110–112, 136, 137
    SD90MAC, 112
Engine type, 112, 113
    Electric, 141
    Four-cycle, 112, 113, 142
    Two-cycle, 112, 113
Ephraim, Max, 45, 113, 157
Eversoll, E.E., 91
Evolution of the Diesel Locomotive in the United States, The, 111

Fairbanks-Morse, 25, 42, 119
Federal Railroad Administration, 154
Ferrier, Wayne, 31
Ferrocarril del Pacifico (FCP), 12, 20, 34, 36, 37, 39, 80, 118, 124
    El Costeño, 21, 36, 37, 80
Ferrocarriles Nacionales Mexicanos (NdeM), 12, 21, 36, 38, 39, 129
    El Tapatio, 38, 39, 129
    GP38 9237, 38
Ferry, Albert, 11
Flemming, Sir Sanford, 11, 12
Franckey, William, 90
Fueling facilities, 61

General Electric (GE), 36, 39, 53, 56, 67, 80, 91, 101, 102, 104, 126, 127, 140, 142–144, 157, 159, 164, 165
    AC, 56, 57, 104, 140
    Dash 7, 127
    Dash 8, 14, 53, 138–140, 164
    Dash 9, 18, 56, 99, 102, 135, 138–140
    P42 GENESIS, 137
    "U-boats", 16, 126
General Motors (GM), 111–113, 117
Gratz, Adam, 90
Great Northern Railway (GN), 11, 113, 114, 142, 143
    Oriental Limited, 142
Grey, Zane, 11

Harriman, E.H., 12
Harrop, Doug, 91, 140, 142
Haverty, Mike, 60
Hayden smelter, 31, 32
Hill, James Jerome, 11, 143
Holley, Noel, 66

Holmes, Gary, 91
Hood, William, 44, 145
Hopkins, Mark, 10, 150
Hunter, Don L., 31
Huntington, Collis, 10

Illecillewaet River, 11
Interstate Commerce Commission, 48, 52

Jacobson, Lowell S. "Jake", 31, 32
Jaehn, Tomas, 10

Krug, Al, 114
Krupp, 137

La Barrancas, 12
Lawson, Gene, 31, 140, 141
Lawson, L. Lloyd, 140, 141
Lima, 111, 114, 115
Little Joe, 64–66, 90, 100, 142, 158
Locomotive Maintenance and Inspection Terminal (LMIT), 78
Locotrol remote-control system, 133

Magma Junction, 31, 32
Marias Pass, 11
McCormick, Doyle, 114
Mexican Central Railroad. *See* Nacionales de Mexico
    Milwaukee's Mighty Electrics, The, 31
Milwaukee Road, 17, 31, 50–52, 62, 64–67, 90, 100, 101, 140, 141, 158–160

167

Milwaukee Road, cont.
   Olympian Hiawatha, 141
   Thunderhawk, 141
   XL Special, 17, 141
Moberly, Walter, 11
Montreal Locomotive Works, 21, 23, 36, 37, 46, 80, 124
   M630, 23, 46, 124
Morrison-Knudsen, 118
Mountain States Contractors, 77

Nathan M5 horn, 42
National Railroad Passenger Corporation. *See* Amtrak
Naugle, J.A., 12
North American Free Trade Agreement, 10
North Coast Railroad Authority, 155
Northwestern Pacific (NWP), 70, 103, 121, 154, 155
Nuehart, Dave, 45, 129

Old Trails National Highway, 29

Powell, Lynn, 91

Railroad shops, 61, 72, 73, 109, 124
Railroaders, 59–87, 89–92, 100, 104, 105
   Jobs, 59–61
   Shifts, 89–92, 100, 104, 105
Railway Age, 113
Road switchers, 120, 121
Rogers, Major Albert B., 12
Rogers Pass, 12

Route 66 "The Mother Road", 29, 30
Ruta de la Costa Occidental, 12
Sacramento Union, 150
Santa Fe Railway, 11, 15, 29, 33, 35, 48, 78, 94, 95, 108, 118, 130–133, 138–140, 144, 145, 149, 153, 157, 164, 165. *See also* Atchison, Topeka & Santa Fe (AT&SF)
Sea-Land, 135
Signals, 90
Simpson, William, 11
Southern Pacific Railroad (SP), 8–10, 12, 20, 23, 26, 30–33, 41, 44, 48, 52–56, 60, 69, 75, 84, 85, 92, 93, 95, 111, 114, 120, 123, 125, 126, 133, 145, 148, 154, 155, 162
   BRLAT (Brooklyn Yard, Oregon–Los Angeles, Trailers), 163
   Daylight, 93
   GS-4, 111
   Harriman, 69
   SSW 9628, 33
   Trainmaster No. 3031, 42
   TRRVY (Tracy, California–Roseville, California, manifest), 120
Stanford, Leland, 10, 150
Stanley, Dave, 91
Stevens, John F., 11, 143
Stevens Pass, 11
Stockton Tower, 130, 131
Styffe, Dave, 91
Sud-Pacifico de Mexico (SPdeM), 12, 36
Sunset magazine, 10, 11

Traffic Control System (TCS), 40
Tunnel Motor, 30, 33, 52, 93, 150

Union Pacific (UP), 12, 18, 28–31, 45, 48, 52, 53, 60, 74, 77, 86–91, 96, 98, 99, 102, 106, 107, 110–112, 127, 129, 130, 135, 140, 142, 157, 167
   Overland Mail West, 91
   LAX, 129
University of Oregon Audiovideo Media Center, 31
Upson, Lauren, 150
U.S. Railroad Administration, 11

Verascal, Robert, 104, 105

Western Pacific (WP), 12, 13, 26, 33, 40, 48, 55, 68, 83, 109, 130, 146, 147
   Exposition Flyer, 55
   WPE, 146
Wheelihan, Jack, 112, 113
Windshield, 114, 115
Winton, 111
   W201A, 112
Winterail, 91
Wipple, Brain, 155
Woodruff, John, 29
Wylie Controller, 66, 90
Wylie, Laurence, 66